Changing Seasons

A Language Arts Curriculum for Healthy Aging

Changing
Seasons

A Language Arts Curriculum for Healthy Aging

❧ Denise L. Calhoun

Purdue University Press, West Lafayette, Indiana

Cataloging-in-Publication Data is on file with the Library of Congress.

Paper ISBN: 978-1-55753-818-5
ePDF ISBN: 978-1-61249-529-3
ePUB ISBN: 978-1-61249-530-9

❧ I strongly believe in the power of the human spirit. If you have the will and the desire, you can accomplish anything at any age. After observing the "changing of the seasons" of my parents, Radford and Earline Knuckles, and my mother-in-law, Jessie Mae Calhoun, I became aware of how important it is to maintain meaningful communication with our older generation. This book is thereby dedicated to them for giving me the inspiration to create a curriculum to help families, staff, and administrators understand the importance of communicating effectively and staying connected with our older family members. ❧

Contents

Acknowledgments

I extend my sincere appreciation to my loving husband, Marion, and wonderful children, Don, Stacy, and Gia, for their love, support, words of wisdom, and insightful comments in helping me create a project of this magnitude. I am also grateful to all of my family members, friends, and professors, Dr. Carrie Rothstein-Fisch and Dr. Bruce Burnam, who have supported me throughout this amazing journey by attending book signings or giving me words of encouragement, guidance, and praise. Finally, I would like to show gratitude to all older adults—past and present—who have paved the way for whatever hopes, dreams, and opportunities we may have for our future.

About the Program

Both communicating and connecting with others are important for sustaining quality of life. Difficulties with communication can lead to social withdrawal and feelings of isolation, dependence, and depression. The purpose of this curriculum is to enrich the quality of life of older adults through participation in a language-based, interdisciplinary program that will help them to improve their communication skills.

According to the Alzheimer's Association in 2018, "a number of studies indicate that maintaining strong social connections and keeping mentally active as we age might lower the risk of cognitive decline and Alzheimer's" ("Prevention and Risk of Alzheimer's and Dementia," https://www.alz.org/research/science/alzheimers_prevention_and_risk.asp). This curriculum provides participants with opportunities to share and connect with others and improve their language and thinking skills by participating in challenging, engaging activities and lessons that encourage active involvement. Its primary use is with non-dementia older adults in assisted-living, nursing home, and adult day services settings as well as senior centers and community groups. However, families can also adapt the curriculum for use with their older adult loved ones.

Curriculum Goals

- Get older adults actively involved in the learning process.
- Build strong communication skills.
- Strengthen cognitive skills through challenging activities that require higher-level (critical) thinking.

- Create an enriched environment to relieve loneliness, depression, and anxiety.
- Assist older adults in establishing and maintaining friendships.
- Increase family involvement.
- Enhance well-being through healthy practices.

Curriculum Content

This language arts curriculum content is divided into two main content areas—oral language and written language—with an emphasis on comprehension. Included are fun warm-up (icebreaker) activities as well as longer activities and lessons.

Some oral language activities involve physical movement or cooking; some writing activities will be ongoing, lasting for several days as participants polish and perfect their poems and essays. Included are fun seasonal and abstract art activities that contain a language arts component.

Curriculum Implementation

As with any educational program, success cannot be met without the support and assistance of family members and, depending on the setting in which it is used, staff and administration. Family members are the best observers of their loved ones' strengths and needs, and they have a sincere interest in their care and welfare. The alliance between families and older adult communities, therefore, not only facilitates effective communication but also promotes quality interaction among participants, staff, and administrators.

However, no matter how great a lesson or an activity might be, it has no value if there is no interest. For administrators, the first step in implementing a program like this one is to build enthusiasm. One way to accomplish this is to point out the benefits of incorporating a language arts curriculum that helps to improve thinking and communication skills. This message could be best communicated via mini-workshops during family night or throughout the day. Implementing the program should be a team effort in which family, staff, and participants work together to make it happen. The main point to emphasize is that language and thinking work hand in hand: language affects thinking and thinking affects language.

After the advantages of the program are reinforced, offer incentives for participants—for example, lottery tickets, senior bucks to buy things in the community, or awards for exemplary work. To acknowledge the work completed, create events that allow participants to show off their accomplishments, such as poetry readings, mock trials to illustrate persuasive writing, gallery walks to view completed projects, and plays—especially whodunits that get the audience actively involved in solving the mystery.

Tips for Facilitators

- Plan ahead. Review the lessons and activities and be prepared. Expect the unexpected. Over time you will get a feel for how long an activity or lesson might take, depending on the makeup of the group.
- Check with participants to make sure they can hear you.
- Be courteous, respectful, patient, encouraging, and supportive.
- Take your time with the activities and lessons. Allow plenty of time for thoughtful responses.
- Practice and model active listening (pay attention, paraphrase what the speaker said, ask questions, and summarize the message) to build rapport, understanding, and trust.
- Keep a positive attitude and remember the saying "Different strokes for different folks." What works for one person or group might not work for another. Find what works.

For best results, consider the population of the community as well as the time frame for other activities planned for the week. It might work best to break the curriculum into segments. Think creatively! You could start a writing club, a book club, a mystery club, or even a Toastmasters-type club. The goal is to encourage older adults to become active learners.

Okay, let's get started!

How to Use This Book

This book is organized into the following sections:

- Oral language activities and lessons: listening (including physical movement and cooking), speaking, and vocabulary building
- Written language activities and lessons: various activities, essays, and poetry
- Seasonal and abstract art activities with a language arts component
- Appendices A, B, and C: supplemental information and materials for activities and lessons
- Appendix D: sample lesson plans to help you get started
- Glossary of oral and written language terminology
- Resource list

Here is a good way to get started:

1. Read the glossary of oral and written language terminology, which will take just a few minutes. This will refresh your memory on terms you learned when you were in school and familiarize you with the glossary contents. You can then refer to it as necessary when preparing for activities and lessons.
2. Activities and lessons are identified with the icon ❧ throughout the book. Read the introductory paragraphs that precede the activities and lessons in each section.
3. Go over the sample lesson plans in appendix D. (See the cross-referenced page numbers for full instructions where indicated.) This will give you a framework for choosing and pairing activities and lessons.

4. Consider the population you are working with and the time frame for other activities planned. Determine what structure would work best and which activities and lessons would appeal the most.

5. When planning lessons, review instructions carefully so you know what materials are required, can anticipate how long the activity/lesson might last, and are mentally prepared to present it. (Note: Some writing activities/lessons will likely last for several days.)

6. Think about ways to display, share, and celebrate work completed. See Curriculum Implementation on p. 2 for some ideas.

7. Set your intention to encourage older adults to become active learners, then enjoy the process!

Oral Language

Oral language involves speaking, listening, questioning, and interpreting tone. The oral language activities and lessons in this curriculum focus on building vocabulary and increasing comprehension. Participants are called upon to employ higher-level thinking skills such as summarizing, predicting, inferring, sequencing, comparing, and contrasting.

Here are three suggestions to help you maintain a relaxed, friendly, and productive atmosphere during oral language lessons and activities:

1. Provide a risk-free environment where participants feel comfortable speaking up.
2. Encourage participants to share their ideas, background knowledge, and experiences and to be responsive and receptive listeners.
3. Provide fair and equitable opportunities for all participants to further develop their speaking and listening skills.

Strategies for Activities and Lessons

- Present instructions one step at a time.
- Slow down. Allow time for participants to think and reflect. Ask them to share their thoughts.
- Reduce the amount of new information presented all at once. Break the information into small bites until you know what participants can handle.
- Use short, simple sentences. Gradually incorporate more complex sentences to stimulate higher-level thinking.
- Repeat and summarize important points.

- Ask participants to repeat what was said in their own words.
- Teach self-questioning strategies to aid memory storage. For example, participants can ask themselves these questions: Can I picture this in my mind? What pops into my head when I hear this? What does this remind me of?
- Stimulate critical (higher-level) thinking by asking who, what, where, when, why, and how questions.
- Encourage participants to share what they know about a topic.
- Encourage construction of full-sentence responses.
- Allow participants to talk about what they know rather than what they don't know. For example, ask:

> What can you say about _____?
> What do you know about _____?
> Tell us about _____.

Some participants might struggle with oral language. The following areas could present difficulties.

- Has trouble pronouncing some words. Speech is difficult to understand. Speech pattern is hesitant and unsure.
- Vocabulary is limited to familiar words. Limits use of new words in spontaneous speech. Has trouble with word associations and categorizations.
- Describes familiar objects rather than calling them by name (e.g., calling a toothbrush a "teeth cleaner"). Buys time to try to retrieve a word by saying "Umm," "Well," or "You know."

Getting Started

The purpose of the following activities is to generate "quality talk." These activities reinforce critical-thinking skills such as predicting, inferring, sequencing, recalling, paraphrasing, analyzing, interpreting, describing, and explaining. They can be used in a variety of ways.

❧ Toss and Talk

Toss and Talk is a great icebreaker to get a group talking without having to volunteer. It can be used as an open-ended sequencing strategy in which each person adds to a story or adds steps to a set of directions when a ball is tossed to him or her. However, the most common use of Toss and Talk involves passing a beach ball covered with fun questions for participants to answer. The ball is passed from one person to another, and the person who receives it answers the question located under his or her right thumb.

❧ Think–Pair–Share

Think–Pair–Share is a learning strategy in which participants work collaboratively to solve a problem or to discuss the answer to a question. The objective is to first think about a topic or response to a question and then share ideas with a partner. This technique allows for maximum participation, focus, and engagement in comprehending information.

❧ Round-Robin

In round-robin reading, participants take turns reading a brief portion of text aloud while the rest of the group follows along in their own copy. In round-robin storytelling, one person starts the story, then in turn others add to it.

❧ Jigsaw

Jigsaw encourages group sharing and for participants to learn specific content. The objective is for participants to share the responsibility for others' learning by using critical-thinking and social skills to complete an assignment. Each person is assigned a selection from a specific text and is tasked to become an expert on that section, and then to teach the other members of his or her group.

Warm-Up Activities

Warm-up activities (icebreakers) should take about 15 minutes. They provide participants an opportunity to connect with other people, build relationships, and share their thoughts and feelings. The following activities can be used on their own or to set up any lesson. Additional warm-up activities are included in the Speaking Lessons section.

❧ Activating Prior Knowledge

This activity builds on background knowledge and experience.

Read a poem or selection from a story or show a picture to trigger memories from the participants' past. Ask the group to respond with their own memories.

❧ Big Little Words

Give the group a big word and see how many little words can be made using letters from the big word. Make a list of all the words found. *Optional:* Give a prize to the person who finds the most little words.

❧ Changing Familiar Songs

Take a familiar song and change it by replacing each verse with a new action to sing and follow. For example, the lyrics "She'll be coming around the mountain when she comes" could be changed to "She'll be swaying side to side when she comes," or "She'll be twisting to the music when she comes." Ask for volunteers to lead the group with a new song.

❧ Describing and Explaining

Start a discussion about something the participants can either describe or explain. For example:

Describe the perfect meal.

Explain how to cook your favorite dish.

Describe the perfect senior community.

Explain the steps of a favorite craft.

Describe a pet peeve. Explain why you find it irritating or annoying.

Describe a favorite place. Explain why it's a favorite.

Describe the perfect mate.

❧ Expressing Opinions

Encourage participants to open up and express their opinion on various topics. For example, ask:

How do you feel about your living conditions?
What can you do to improve your quality of life?
What makes a good leader?
What makes you happy, sad, or mad?

❧ FAVORITES

Ask for one sentence or thought from each person about his or her favorite thing. Provide the option of saying more if that feels comfortable. Some suggestions are favorite store, music, foods, places, sports, dances, restaurants, animals, presidents, books, characters, TV shows, desserts, flowers, and time of life.

❧ FIRSTS

Every person has had and has done many things for first time: first pet, first love, first school, first home, first job. Ask questions to generate discussions that bring back memories and activate prior knowledge.

A variation is to have participants think of phrases that incorporate firsts:
First comes the puppy, then the [dog].
First comes the seed, then the [tree].
First comes the tadpole, then the [frog].
First comes the smile, then the [friend].

❧ GUESS WHO

Describe a participant first by physical appearance and then by personality traits. Have the group guess who was described.

❧ IMAGINATION

Encourage participants to tap into their imagination. For example, ask:
What will the world be like in 100 years?
What if you found out that the house you live in is haunted?
If you could take a trip to the moon, what would you bring?
If you had a million dollars to spend in one day, what would you buy?
If you could change one thing in the world, what would it be and why?
Where would you go if you could visit anywhere in the world?
If you could sail around the world, what countries would you visit?

❧ Keepsakes

Ask the group to each bring in a favorite object, hidden in a bag. (Have extra bags available.) Taking turns, participants provide three descriptive clues about their object (e.g., texture, color, shape, size, sound). They also may answer questions about their object, such as: How long have you had it? Where did you get it? Why do you treasure it? The group tries to guess what the object is.

❧ Paraphrasing

Here are two fun paraphrasing activities:
- Read a poem or selection from a story, then ask for a volunteer to paraphrase the selection.
- Show a picture and ask a participant to describe it. Then, ask for a volunteer to paraphrase the description.

❧ Picture Guessing

Select a picture from a stack of picture cards and describe it. Call on the group to guess what it is. Have the group take turns selecting and describing a picture.

❧ Recounting Experiences

Ask the participants to share events or milestones in their lives. Possible topics:
Your earliest memory.
When you were a child. . . .
Something that made you happy or sad.
If you could change one thing in your life. . . .

❧ Self-Esteem

Lead a discussion that helps build self-esteem. Help participants feel comfortable talking about themselves by asking questions such as:
How would you describe yourself?
What is your best quality?
What are you an expert at doing?
What would you like to learn? Why?
What traits do you admire in others? Why?

When do you feel special?

How can others help you?

What makes a good friend?

❧ SEQUENCING

Read a story to the group, then have the group members retell the story. This can be done in a round-robin session with everyone seated in a circle. Another option is to draw numbers to determine the order. Choose one person to be the recorder. As each person tells the story, the recorder writes down the responses. After everyone has had a turn, the recorder reads the responses to the group. Next, reread the story, comparing it to the recorder's notes to confirm that the details are in sequence.

❧ SWAPPING STORIES AND JOKES

This activity gives participants an opportunity to share stories or memorable events from their lives. Ask participants to:

Tell a funny story about themselves.

Talk about a book they have read or currently are reading.

Tell a joke or riddle.

Share something funny that happened to them since they have been in this community.

A variation is to create a yarn story. Give a ball of yarn to one person to start the story. After making up the beginning of the story, the first person passes the yarn to the next person, who continues the story. Participants continue adding to the story until everyone has had a turn. The last person handed the yarn provides an ending to the story.

❧ TONGUE TWISTERS

Tongue twisters are great for strengthening articulation. A fun activity is to see how many times a person can repeat a tongue twister in an allotted amount of time. Following are a few popular tongue twisters, but have fun making up your own.

"A big black bee bit a big black bear and made a big black bear bleed blood."

"Peter Piper picked a peck of pickled peppers. How many pickled peppers did Peter Piper pick?"

"How much wood could a woodchuck chuck, if a woodchuck could chuck
wood?"

"Rubber baby buggy bumpers."

"She sells seashells by the seashore."

✺ VIDEO INTERPRETATION

Play a short video without the sound, pausing periodically to ask the group
what is happening or what might happen next. After viewing the entire video,
discuss the group's predictions, including why things did or didn't happen
as predicted. Show the entire video again, uninterrupted and with sound.

✺ WORD BOX

Create an attractive box and place it in an easily accessible location, along
with index cards and pens or pencils. Invite participants and staff members
to write new or interesting words onto the cards and drop them into the word
box. Throughout the day, pull a card from the word box while in a public
space, or announce the word over the building loudspeaker. Participants earn
rewards by responding with the correct definition of the word. If the activity
is conducted in a public space, encourage a discussion of the word with the
people present.

A variation of the activity is to create a questionnaire to find out favorite
songs from different eras and genres—for example, music from the '40s, '50s,
'60s, '70s; Classical, Country, R&B, Blues, Jazz, Rock; Frank Sinatra, Elvis
Presley, Johnny Mathis, The Platters, Nat King Cole. Make a card for each
favorite song and then, throughout the day, pick a song from the box to play
or to sing with the group.

Lessons

The oral language lessons provided here are organized into three areas: listening, speaking, and vocabulary building. The objective is for participants
to be able to listen with comprehension and speak clearly.

Listening

One way to assess and improve listening ability is through lessons that require participants to follow directions. Another is through activities that require recall and paraphrasing. The first set of lessons in this section are on following oral directions and include simple recipes. The remaining lessons require participants to solve mysteries, predict endings, and respond to a passage from a selection of fine literature. These lessons include step-by-step directions or directed instructions and can include guided practice, independent activities, and extended activities.

Directed instruction is used when teaching a new concept or skill. It often includes modeling a variety of examples and guiding participants during their review and practice.

Guided practice is interactive instruction between the facilitator and participants. After introducing a new activity, the facilitator begins the practice process by engaging participants in a task similar to the one they will complete independently.

During *independent practice* or *activity,* participants practice the concept or skills presented during instruction to work toward mastery.

Extended activities allow the facilitator to vary or extend the lesson.

Following Oral Directions

❧ Beading Necklaces

Given an oral description of each bead, participants create a necklace with a specific pattern.

Guided Practice

Have the group practice listening to the description of various beads and locating them in a pile. A variation is to have the group practice describing beads by placing a number of beads in a baggie and having each participant pull out one and describe it to the group.

Independent Activity
1. Provide each person with a small baggie of decorative beads and a 16-inch-long string for beading.
2. Inform the group that each participant is creating a necklace. (If time is short, have the group create bracelets.)
3. The objective is to string the beads in the order given, based on the description.
4. Remind the participants to listen very carefully to be able choose the correct bead.
5. After the activity is complete, each person has the option of keeping the design (you can add a clasp) or creating his or her own pattern.

❧ Follow My Lead
Given oral directions, participants draw a picture.

Directed Instruction
1. Display a few simple drawings or pictures.
2. Have the group decide which picture they would like to draw.
3. Display the picture and model step by step how to draw it.
4. Keeping the picture displayed, have the group draw the picture following your verbal cues.

Independent Activity
Instruct the group to follow your lead. Give oral directions for creating a simple drawing. For example, to draw a rectangle:
1. Draw two parallel vertical lines the same length.
2. Draw a horizontal line connecting the bottom endpoints.
3. Draw a parallel horizontal line connecting the top endpoints.

As the participants become more adept at following your lead, you can give them more complex pictures to draw.

Extended Activity: Squiggle Wiggle Drawings
Give simple oral directions to draw squiggle designs. For example:

Make these lines:

1. zigzag,
2. zigzag,   *Me*
3. curve up and around, then down.

Have participants take turns creating squiggle designs on chart paper or a whiteboard and giving directions to the group. The group tries to recreate the design by paying close attention to the directions.

TOTAL PHYSICAL RESPONSE (TPR)

Given commands using directional words, participants follow oral directions.

Guided Practice

- Call out exercises using directional words. For example: "Bend your right arm up and down; twist your left foot counterclockwise."
- Add music to give the exercises more flair.

Independent Activities

- Have participants take turns giving directions.
- A variation is to present open-ended directions: "What part of your body can go up and down? What can bend . . . twist . . . slide . . . stretch . . . shake . . . move back and forth or side to side?"

Extended Activity: Clapping Rhythmic Patterns

- Model various rhythmic patterns by clapping and instruct the group to copy the pattern.
- This activity is not limited to clapping. Demonstrate using other parts of the body to illustrate patterns (e.g., snapping fingers, shaking the head, moving shoulders up and down).
- A variation is to give each person a different rhythmic instrument to produce the pattern. Have the group take turns producing patterns.

Following Simple Recipe Steps

The goal is for participants to follow oral instructions and make a simple snack. Start off with recipes that have simple directions, then over time move on to those with more complex directions.

Provide choices of two or three recipes for a simple snack. Make sure the choices have many of the same ingredients. Once a recipe is chosen, put all ingredients in a basket, minus the spices, then follow these steps.

1. Provide each person with the kitchen tools (utensils, bowls, plates, etc.) needed to complete the meal.
2. Read the list of ingredients to the group.
3. Pass the basket of ingredients around and instruct the participants to gather the required ingredients.
4. After the ingredients are distributed, give the directions one step at a time.
5. Ask the participants to repeat the directions one at a time, and then begin making the snack.
6. After the snack is complete, eat and enjoy!

Recipes should be for no-cook snacks that participants can prepare and eat in one sitting and should serve one or two people. Simple recipes are provided here. (See appendix A for additional recipes, some of which require a microwave, oven, or refrigeration.)

⚜ Tasty Magic Wands
Ingredients list for each participant
    2 pretzel rods
    ⅓ cup chopped nuts, dried fruit, and/or crushed frosty flakes cereal
    Peanut butter to taste
Directions
    1. Spread peanut butter on a few inches of the pretzel rod.
    2. Roll the rods in chopped nuts, dried fruit, or frosty flakes. (Mixing and matching is fun and tasty, too!)

❧ Apple Crescent Treats
Ingredients list for each participant

   1 apple
   ⅓ cup granola
   Peanut butter to taste
   Honey to taste

Directions

   1. Slice apples into crescents.
   2. Spread with peanut butter.
   3. Press granola on top.
   4. Drip honey over granola.

❧ Crackerberries
Ingredients list for each participant

   8 saltine crackers
   4 strawberries
   1 tablespoon honey
   Peanut butter to taste

Directions

   1. Spread peanut butter on saltines.
   2. Cut strawberries into thin slices.
   3. Place cut strawberries on saltines.
   4. Drizzle with honey.

❧ Banana Butter Trail Mix
Ingredients list for each participant

   ½ banana
   ¼ cup trail mix
   Peanut butter to taste

Directions

   1. Cut banana into quarters and lay flat on a plate.
   2. Spread peanut butter on banana quarters.
   3. Sprinkle trail mix on top.

✺ Peanutty Rice Cakes

Ingredients list for each participant

1 rice cake

1 tablespoon toasted shredded coconut

2 teaspoons dried cherries

Peanut butter to taste

Directions

1. Spread peanut butter on rice cake.
2. Sprinkle with toasted shredded coconut.
3. Add dried cherries.

✺ Pineapple Celery Sticks

Ingredients list for each participant

3 stalks celery

4 ounces cream cheese

¼ cup crushed pineapple

Directions

1. Cut celery stalks in half.
2. Drain crushed pineapple.
3. Mix pineapple and cream cheese in a bowl.
4. Stuff celery with mixture.

Ask participants what else they think might be good for stuffing celery.

✺ Jicama Chili Sticks

Ingredients list for each participant

1 jicama

¼ lime

Chili powder to taste

Directions

1. Peel the jicama.
2. Cut jicama into manageable pieces (approximately 3 × ½ × ½ inches) and place on a paper towel.
3. Squeeze lime juice over jicama.
4. Sprinkle with chili powder.
5. Arrange on plate and serve cold.

❧ Pear Salad Animal Faces

Ingredients list for each participant

- 1 lettuce leaf
- 1 tangerine
- 1 canned pear half
- 1 large or 2 small grapes (red or purple)
- 1 maraschino cherry

Directions

1. Place lettuce leaf on plate.
2. Place canned pear half, cut side down, on lettuce.
3. Peel tangerine and use 4 sections for ears.
4. Cut large grape in half and use as eyes. (If grapes are small, use the whole grape.)
5. Cut cherry into 6 slices and use for nose or whiskers and mouth.

Pear Salad Animal Faces

❧ Hummus Sticks

Ingredients list for each participant

- 1 celery stalk
- ¼ cup hummus
- 3 olives (green, black, or Kalamata)

Directions

1. Cut celery stalk evenly lengthwise into 3 sections.
2. Stuff each section with hummus.
3. Slice olives in quarters.
4. Top each celery section with 4 olive slices.

⤳ Fruit Salad Tree

Ingredients list for each participant

1 lettuce leaf

1 slice pineapple

½ banana

Sliced fresh fruit or 1 small can fruit cocktail

Grapes

Directions

1. Place lettuce leaf on plate.
2. Place slice of pineapple in center of lettuce.
3. Place banana vertically in center of pineapple.
4. Drain fruit cocktail.
5. Put fruit cocktail and grapes on toothpicks.
6. Arrange skewered fruit on banana.
7. Ask participants to think of other salads they could make with fruit.

FRUIT SALAD TREE

❧ APPLE CARROT SALAD

Ingredients list for each participant

1 carrot

2 apples

½ cup raisins

⅓ cup mayonnaise

1 teaspoon lemon juice

Directions

1. Peel carrot and apples.
2. Grate carrot and apples in a bowl.
3. Add ⅓ cup mayonnaise.
4. Add lemon juice.
5. Mix gently.

❧ FIBER FRUIT PARFAIT

Ingredients list for each participant

1½ cup fiber cereal, divided in half

6 ounces low-fat yogurt, divided in half

¼ cup blueberries, divided in half

½ cup strawberries, sliced and divided in half

Directions

Layer half of each ingredient in the order given (see illustration next page).

1. Place half of the cereal in a dessert dish.
2. Layer half of the yogurt on top of the cereal.
3. Mix remaining half of the cereal with half of the sliced strawberries and half of the blueberries.
4. Layer this mixture on top of the yogurt.
5. Layer remaining half of the yogurt on top of mixture.
6. Mix remaining strawberries and blueberries.
7. Layer this mixture on top of yogurt.

FIBER FRUIT PARFAIT

Within the bowl:

Top: strawberries and blueberries

Next: yogurt

Next: cereal, blueberries and strawberries

Next: yogurt

Bottom: cereal

❧ BANANA NUT YOGURT

Ingredients list for each participant

- ½ cup plain yogurt
- ¼ cup chopped banana
- 1–2 tablespoons sugar
- 2–3 tablespoons of chopped nuts (walnuts, pecans, almonds, or cashews)
- 1 tablespoon honey

Directions

1. Mix yogurt and sugar in serving bowl.
2. Add banana to yogurt mixture.
3. Top with nuts.
4. Drizzle honey over nuts.

Solving Mysteries, Predicting Endings, and
Responding to Fine Literature

❧ SOLVING MYSTERIES

Given a mystery or crime scene scenario and clues, participants work together to solve a mystery.

1. Each participant chooses his or her favorite mystery to present to the group.
2. The participant presents the scenario to the group and points out the clues.
3. The group works together or breaks up into smaller groups to solve the mystery.

❧ PREDICTING ENDINGS

Participants predict or change endings to stories.

Directed Instruction

1. Introduce a new novel or short story to the group.
2. Read one chapter at a time without giving away the chapter ending. Ask critical-thinking questions as you read.
3. Brainstorm ideas for the chapter or story ending.
4. Read the ending, then compare and contrast with group predictions.
5. Repeat the process for remaining chapters.

❧ RESPONDING TO FINE LITERATURE

After listening to excerpts from a novel, short story, or poem, participants paraphrase, interpret, or recall text.

Guided Practice

1. Use a famous quote — for example, this quote widely attributed to Mark Twain: "Age is an issue of mind over matter. If you don't mind, it doesn't matter."
2. Practice recalling and reciting the quote.
3. Brainstorm interpretations of the quote (e.g., ask: What point do you think the person reciting this quote is trying to convey?).

Directed Instruction

Read a passage from a story or a poem of interest to the group—for example, "Nothing Gold Can Stay" by Robert Frost.

> Nature's first green is gold,
> Her hardest hue to hold.
> Her early leaf's a flower;
> But only so an hour.
> Then leaf subsides to leaf.
> So Eden sank to grief,
> So dawn goes down to day.
> Nothing gold can stay.

Line 1, "Nature's first green is gold," provides the setting of the poem and makes the reader think about spring. The first green is actually gold; for example, willow trees, which are golden in early spring before they mature to green. Or maybe the line refers to morning, when the sun rises and the light of dawn makes everything look a little more golden.

Line 2 could mean that nature is gold before it is green. Gold is the hardest hue, or color, for nature to maintain, which is why the first color we see in spring doesn't last very long. (The idea of nature having an easy or hard time holding onto something is an example of *personification*.)

In line 3, "Her early leaf's a flower" could mean that, just as nature's first green is gold, her first leaf is a flower. In spring, trees and bushes bloom with gorgeous flowers, which are replaced by green leaves in the summer.

The line "So Eden sank to grief" could be comparing humankind's expulsion from the Garden of Eden to the change from gold with green described in the first half of the poem. Just like the flowers subsided, or were downgraded to become leaves, Eden also sinks, referring to the fall of Adam and Eve. When Eve ate the forbidden fruit, she and Adam as well as all of their descendants were forever punished by being banished from Eden and were subject to all the grief that humans experience today. This line also could refer to childhood. When someone is young and innocent the world is beautiful, just like nature in the spring. Nothing of our youth lasts forever, however—once we get older we view the world differently.

These are all possible interpretations. The goal, however, is to encourage participants to come up with their own ideas about what the writer is trying to convey.

After reading the poem to the group, break it down line by line. Sample questions and responses for "Nothing Gold Can Stay" are provided here:

Q: The first line gives the setting. What season does it make you think of?
A: Spring.
Q: How can the first green be gold?
A: Some trees, such as willow trees, are golden in early spring. Or perhaps because it is early morning—when the sun first rises and everything appears to have a slight gold tint.
Q: What is meant by the line "So Eden sank to grief"?
A: It references the Bible: humankind's expulsion from the Garden of Eden.
Q: What do you think the poem means?
A: *Accept all ideas.* You might be surprised by how creative each person is. The objective is to get the group to interact by acknowledging the ideas of their peers.

Read the poem again. As a group, try to paraphrase each line.

SPEAKING

People like to talk about what they know and love. Appendix B contains sample questionnaires you can use to help you get to know your group, which will help you to plan activities and lessons that everyone will enjoy.

When developing speaking lessons, incorporate critical-thinking questions that ask who, what, when, why, and how. For example:

What would happen if...?
Why do you think that...?
How would you solve...?
Who do you think is best for...?

Would it be better if. . . ?

Can you give an example. . . ?

Can you elaborate on the reason. . . ?

Can you explain. . . ?

What would you recommend. . . ?

What would it be like if. . . ?

What can you conclude. . . ?

When do you think that would be appropriate. . . ?

The main objective for speaking lessons is to provide a clear structure for group work that requires everyone to participate and speak. It is the responsibility of the facilitator to work with each group to monitor and encourage participation.

Participation should be meaningful, purposeful, and cognitively appropriate. Lessons should also include socialization and interaction; integrating and evaluating information presented in diverse media and formats; and reasoning and analyzing a speaker's point of view.

The first lessons should emphasize the following basics:

- ✓ Articulating (expressing oneself clearly and effectively)
- ✓ Looking at the audience
- ✓ Speaking with the intent of being heard by others
- ✓ Answering questions from the audience
- ✓ Speaking without fidgeting

These can be learned through reciting poems, raps, and chants; role-playing; participating in plays or skits; and singing songs. The rhyme and rhythm of songs, raps, chants, and poems appeal to many. And you can incorporate movement with each.

People are more willing to join in when they are a part of a larger group. This gives hesitant speakers an opportunity to participate without feeling intimidated. Below are warm-up/icebreaker activities, followed by facilitator-directed lessons.

Warm-Up Activities

The following activities can be used on their own or to set up any lesson.

✺ BALL TOSS

- Toss a lightweight ball or beanbag to a participant, asking him or her to recall an important concept, repeat a line in a poem, or explain material presented.
- This exercise is also effective for building sentences. Start by volleying a ball to create simple sentences and then transition into adding adjectives and connecting words.
- Another variation to is to complete sentences. Start a sentence (e.g., My favorite job was. . . . I am happy when. . . .) and toss the ball to someone to complete it.

✺ CAT IN THE HAT

This activity fosters interpersonal empathy.

1. Each participant anonymously writes a feeling, concern, or pet peeve on a slip of paper and folds it up. A volunteer collects the folded slips of paper in a bowl.
2. Each participant randomly draws a piece paper, reads it to the group, then interprets how the person might feel.
3. The group then discusses the person's feelings or concerns.

✺ HUMAN BINGO

1. Make a large Bingo card (5 by 5).
2. At the top of each square, write a characteristic—something that someone in the group is or has done (e.g., has great-grandchildren; is more than 70 years old; got married in the spring).
3. Give each participant a copy of the card.
4. Participants circulate to talk with others and have them sign one square that is true of them.
5. The first person to fill all squares wins.

❧ Jigsaw Activities

These activities enable participants to learn concepts without having to read dense and lengthy text. They also provide opportunities for everyone to speak.

1. Participants sit in groups of four and count off from 1 to 4.
2. The groups read the introduction and one section of the text together.
3. Divide up the rest of the text and have each person read his or her section silently:

   Number 1s read section 1.

   Number 2s read section 2.

   Number 3s read section 3.

   Number 4s read section 4.
4. Participants gather with others who have read the same section (1s meet with 1s, 2s with 2s, etc.) to form "expert" groups.
5. Expert groups discuss the section they read and compile a list of key points.
6. Everyone returns to their original group and briefly summarizes and explains their section to the group.

A variation is to chart the information for each section and conduct a gallery walk, where participants circulate to view and discuss the charts. To add flair, play classical music as the group walks around reviewing the charts.

❧ Lucky Penny

1. Provide a coin to each participant.
2. Participants take turns revealing the date on their coin and recalling something eventful that happened that year. It can be personal or a world event.

❧ Pantomime

1. Participants take turns pantomiming something of interest (e.g., describe a meal, an outing, or a scene from a movie).
2. The group tries to guess what it is.

Stand Up/Pair Up
1. Select a topic of interest or a skill the group is working on.
2. Direct the group to move around to the sound of music.
3. Stop the music (as in Musical Chairs) and guide everyone to find a partner.
4. Partners discuss the selected topic for five minutes, taking notes and reporting back to the group if desired.
5. Repeat the process with the same or a different topic, depending on the group, instructing the group to find a different partner when the music stops.

Storytelling
1. Sit in a circle.
2. Start a story by showing a picture or using an opening sentence (e.g., One day. . . . One scary night. . . .).
3. Going around the circle (round-robin), each person adds a sentence to the story after repeating the sentence that was just added.

To Tell the Truth
1. Participants write down two truths and one lie about themselves.
2. In turn, each person introduces the three "facts" to the group.
3. The group tries to guess which one is a lie.

Facilitator-Directed Lessons

Acknowledging Others' Points of View
Participants show respect for others' points of view.

Directed Instruction
1. Present a topic that will interest the group.
2. Discuss ways to share ideas respectfully.
3. Present sentence frames:
   I agree with because. . . .
   My thoughts are similar or related to because. . . .
   My partner pointed out that. . . .
   _____ emphasized that. . . .

We share the same idea about. . . .

We disagree on _____.

4. Practice discussing and sharing ideas as a group by incorporating sentence frames.

Independent Practice

1. Have everyone team up with a partner.
2. Give each team a different topic and time to discuss. Examples:

    What if you had to leave your family and country of birth and walk 50 miles to cross an international border?

    What if you had to learn about a new country (its language and culture) and find a job to earn money to send to your family back home?

    After reading a short story: What is the character's point of view? What is the narrator's point of view?

3. Teams will share their topic with the group, being mindful of acknowledging their partner's point of view.

❧ THE MAGIC WAND

Participants learn about the desires and frustrations of others.

Directed Instruction

1. Tell the group: You have just found a magic wand that allows you to make three community-related changes. You can change anything you want—for example, physical appearance, activities, staffing, food, rules.
2. Brainstorm possible changes to make.
3. Chart changes using a graphic organizer, such as a word web, tree map, circle map, or list. (See appendix C for templates.)

Independent Practice

1. Divide participants into three groups.
2. Assign each group a different community-related change.
3. The groups choose someone to be the recorder, then discuss why their change is important. The recorder illustrates the change by charting the information using a graphic organizer if desired.

4. The groups come up with three reasons the community would benefit from their change.
5. Construct a mini-report to present to the administration.

❧ Debatable Discussions
Participants show respect for others' opinions and sharpen their debate skills.

Directed Instruction
1. Choose a simple topic that everyone can relate to (e.g., older adults staying in the workforce longer).
2. Work as a group to create a list of pros and cons.
3. After the list is compiled, brainstorm reasons for each pro and con.
4. Divide the group into pros and cons.
5. Choose a neutral person to be a referee.
6. Conduct a mock debate.

Independent Practice
1. Provide a topic for a debate. For example:
   Women are more detail oriented than men
   Children should be seen and not heard
   Having many friends is better than having one best friend
2. Each member of the group chooses a side—pro or con.
3. Each group prepares its defense.
4. Bring in people to listen to and judge the debate.

❧ Conducting Interviews
Participants get to know each other better.

Directed Instruction
1. Either prepare questions ahead of time or brainstorm questions as a group to provide general guidelines. Suggested questions include those about family life, past jobs, hobbies, or a favorite sport.

2. Have participants partner with someone they do not know well and interview each other for about 15 minutes, recording responses.
3. Give partners another 15 minutes to design creative name tags. The tags can include hobbies, pictures, and/or a self-profile.
4. Reassemble the group and have everyone introduce their partner.

Extended Activity: Create a Dictionary
1. Use interview responses to write a dictionary definition for each person. For example, Smith, Mary: (a) married, (b) three children, (c) from California, (d) loves dancing.
2. Bind all definitions in a book.

✥ IMAGINARY BALL (WORD ASSOCIATION)
Participants think, listen, and pay attention to details.

Instructions
1. Have the group sit in a circle.
2. Choose one person to hold an imaginary ball.
3. That person says the name of another person in the group, then "tosses the ball" to that person while saying the first word that comes to mind. For example, "heart." The person who catches the ball then says a word associated with that word (e.g., "valentine," "love," "beat").
4. The group continues tossing the ball and making word associations until everyone has had a turn.

✥ MEMORIES
Participants talk about favorite memories. This activity requires dice: one die for each participant.

Instructions
1. Choose an era for each number on the die. For example, '50s = 1, '60s = 2, '70s = 3, and so forth.

2. Have the group take turns rolling their die and thinking of a memory from the corresponding era.
3. Ask the following questions about the memory:
   What time of year was it?
   What scents were in the air?
   Where were you?
   Who was with you?
   How did you feel?
   What made this day different?

Vary the activity by choosing another topic, such as happiest time, proudest moment, best vacation, first love, most embarrassing moment.

Vocabulary Building

Oral language has an important social function. It helps us to share our thoughts and feelings, connect with others, and build relationships. Oral language skills are enhanced through building a vocabulary. In this curriculum, vocabulary building is accomplished through activities and games that help participants become more aware of the characteristics, usage, and origins of words.

Root Words

Many English words have origins in Greek or Latin. Learning the roots of words can increase vocabulary, and it helps those who have memory problems. The following are examples of common root words.

Audi/Aud: Hear (e.g., auditorium, audience, audition, audible)
Cede: To go, to yield (e.g., succeed, exceed, proceed, precede)
Chron: Time (e.g., anachronism, chronological; to have events arranged in the order they occurred)
Crede: To believe (e.g., credible, incredible)

Cycle: Wheel (e.g., cyclical, encyclopedia, cycle, bicycle)

Cyclo: Circle (e.g., bicycle, cyclical, cycle, encyclopedia)

Demo: People (e.g., democracy, epidemic, demographic)

Dict: To speak (e.g., diction; a person's manner of speaking)

Extra: Outside; something that is outside the usual (e.g., extraordinary)

Inter: Between (e.g., international, intermittent, intercept, intermission)

Multi: Many (e.g., multitude, multiply)

Script: To write (e.g., inscription)

Tract: To drag, to draw (e.g., traction, attractive, subtraction, tractor)

Vita: Life (e.g., vital, vitality; something essential to organic life)

Sample Activities for Learning Root Words

- Divide the group into two teams. Assign a root for the group. Have each team make a list of as many words as possible that contain that root. For example, *act:* action, react, actor, transact.
- Create a die naming the roots of words. Have participants take turns rolling the die and giving a new word for each root. Have someone be the recorder and make a list of each new word.
- Create a Bingo card that uses the roots of words. Given the definition of the root of a word, participants play Bingo by placing their marker on the correct root.
- Pull words from a box or bag and pantomime or gesture the word.

The History of Words

Knowing the history or story behind a word can help us remember and understand the word. Some words are based on myths or legends of the ancient Greeks and Romans, and many others are derivatives from other languages. The name of a character may illustrate the trait or legend so well that the character's name becomes that idea or trait.

The more we know about a word's origin, the more easily we remember the word. Following are some examples.

Words from Myths and Legends

Ceres

History: The Roman goddess of corn and agriculture. She gave humans the gift of the earth.

Definition: Cereal—a breakfast food prepared from wheat, oats, or corn.

Echo

History: Tragic nymph who fell in love with a beautiful young man who didn't love her; she then only could repeat what was said to her. She stayed in a cave and withered away until only her voice was left.

Definition: Repetition of a sound produced by the reflection of sound waves off a surface.

The Fates

History: The three goddesses who determine the length and course of every aspect of life. One spins the thread of a person's life, another measures it, and the third cuts it.

Definition: Fatality—necessity; a death caused by disaster.

The Furies

History: The three terrible and fierce spirits that have wings and have snakes for hair. They punish people who commit crimes, pursuing them until they become insane.

Definition: Fury—violent; anger or rage.

Janus

History: The Roman god of beginnings and endings. He has two faces—one that looks forward and one that looks backward.

Definition: January—the first month of the year.

Jove or Jupiter

History: The ruler of the Roman gods who is called Zeus by the Greeks. He causes storm clouds and throws thunderbolts when he is angry, but he is also thought of as a source of happiness.

Definition: Jovial—cheerful and full of good humor.

Labyrinth

History: In Greek mythology, a monster called the Minotaur was confined in a labyrinth.

Definition: A maze; a series of complicated passages where it is easy to get lost.

Mars

History: The Roman god of war who particularly enjoys violent battles.

Definition: Martial—relating to war or soldiers.

Mentor

History: A character in the epic tale the *Odyssey.* A wise teacher and counselor who is a friend to the hero, Odysseus, and a teacher to his son.

Definition: Mentor—a wise teacher, guide, or advisor.

Mercury

History: The messenger of the gods, he wears winged sandals and moves gracefully and quickly.

Definition: Mercurial—quick and changeable in temper.

The Muses

History: The nine beautiful goddesses who look after the different arts and sciences.

Definition: Muse—the spirit that inspires someone, especially a writer, musician, or artist.

Odyssey

History: An ancient epic poem that describes the wanderings of Odysseus as he spends 10 years trying to return home from battle after the fall of Troy.

Definition: Odyssey—a long wandering; a difficult journey or trip.

Pan

History: The Greek god of woodlands and wild animals. He has horns, the legs of a goat, and a human torso and head. Supposedly, he is responsible for strange sounds heard in the night.

Definition: Panic—a sudden feeling of terror or fright.

Psyche

History: In Greek mythology, Psyche is a nymph who represents the spirit.

Definition: Psychology—the science of mind and behavior.

Sirens

History: Sea nymphs that lure sailors to their death. These half-bird and half-woman creatures sing a beautiful song that causes sailors to turn their boats toward it and crash on the rocks.

Definition: A device that makes a loud sound; any warning signal.

The Titans

    History: The race of giants. Although they had enormous size and incredible strength in their favor, they were defeated by the Greek Olympians.

    Definition: Titan, titanic—of great size, strength, or power.

Vulcan

    History: The Roman god of fire and forge. This blacksmith forged armor for other gods and heroes. He is known for his skill at metal working.

    Definition: Vulcanize—to harden or change by great heat.

Words Taken from Other Languages

Many English words are taken from other languages. Besides knowing the history of words, being aware of their foreign origin can help to build vocabulary. Following are some examples.

Admiral: Commander of ships (Old French, Medieval Latin, Arabic)

Algebra: Summing up (Medieval Latin from Arabic)

Denim: A coarse fabric used for jeans (French)

Eureka: Exclamation of surprise (Greek)

Faux pas: False step (French)

Finale: End (Italian)

Gourmet: Connoisseur of fine food and wine (French)

Kangaroo: Large hopping animal (Australian Aboriginal)

Menu: A list of a restaurant's foods (French)

Mesa: Tableland or small high plateau (Spanish)

Mustache: Hair under nose (French, Italian, Greek)

Pajamas: Clothes for sleeping (Hindi and Urdu from Persian)

Parka: Heavy coat (Russian)

Patio: Porch (Spanish)

Safari: Trip to see animals (Arabic)

Sherbet/Sherbert: Frozen fruit dessert (Turkish and Persian)

Thespian: An actor (Greek)

Tortilla: Flat bread (Spanish)

Typhoon: Great wind (Chinese; also Portuguese from Arabic and Greek)

Activities Using New Vocabulary

❧ BOARD GAMES
Create board games for new vocabulary words.
1. Draw a path and mark off spaces.
2. Add a vocabulary word to each space.
3. A player rolls the dice to see how many spaces to move.
4. The player provides the definition and origin of the word in the space landed on.

❧ INCOMPLETE SENTENCES
Take turns completing sentences orally. Construct sentences that indicate a word's meaning, such as:

It's fun to be at a jovial event because _____.
A dinosaur is a titanic animal because _____.
What would make a person shout "Eureka!"? _____
New activities directors might need a mentor because _____.
A makeup artist might need a muse because _____.
Fatalities might occur when _____.
The politician felt the fury of the people when _____.

As a variation, list words on a chart and provide a point value for each word. Give participants an incomplete sentence and ask them to find the word on the chart that completes the sentence.

❧ MATCHING PREFIXES AND SUFFIXES
1. Color-code index cards with prefixes, suffixes, and meanings.
2. Match prefixes with correct meaning.
3. Match suffixes with correct meaning.

❧ RECALLING WORDS
1. Write prefixes and suffixes on index cards.
2. Separate cards into suffix and prefix piles.

3. Have participants or groups draw from one pile and think of a word containing that prefix or suffix. Give extra points if a player is able to use the word in a sentence.

❧ WRITING DESCRIPTIONS FOR ORAL PRESENTATION

Have participants write three- or four-line descriptions using new words learned, then present them to the group. For example:

> Describe an imaginary person or someone in your life who has been a mentor.
> Describe a character in a book or movie who is mercurial.
> Describe something that is titanic.

Grammar and Word Usage

Adjectives

Using the wrong word can generate negative feelings. Different words work for different audiences. Following is a list of powerful adjectives.

ample	exceptional	phenomenal	tranquil
appealing	exuberant	quintessential	tremendous
awesome	fascinating	splendid	unquestionable
breathtaking	first-class	stunning	vivid
brilliant	marvelous	tempting	worthwhile

The following adjectives can be used in activities to describe a person's feelings.

affable	confident	glorious	sad
annoyed	depressed	gratified	shy
apprehensive	eager	intense	silly
blissful	ecstatic	melancholy	tickled
cheerful	embarrassed	positive	upset

Synonyms

Synonyms play a very powerful role in building and expanding vocabulary. Participants should be encouraged to make their own personal thesaurus. Along with creating board games and completing sentences to demonstrate understanding of synonyms, activities include identifying words from a list that have the same meaning.

❧ Identifying Synonyms

The following list can help to get the activity started. Participants identify the synonyms for each main word. Extend the activity by giving extra points if the person can provide a synonym for the word that does not belong in the group (the underlined words—antonyms—in the following list).

successful: thriving triumphant flourishing destitute
weird: odd bizarre unusual ordinary
evil: diabolical virtuous malevolent heinous
special: exceptional novel mediocre unique
important: crucial momentous inconsequential imperative
clean: contaminated immaculate pristine tidy
warm: affectionate compassionate apathetic tender
active: energetic animated vigorous dormant
cranky: irritable amiable cantankerous fractious
busy: engaged industrious occupied indolent

As a variation, play Hangman using new vocabulary words. Also, try other activities, such as Bingo or word association.

❧ Hangman

1. One player thinks of a word or phrase and draws a blank line for each letter (e.g., animated = _ _ _ _ _ _ _ _).
2. The other players try to guess the word or phrase one letter at a time (e.g., Is there an "m"?)
3. If a player guesses correctly, then the letter is written in the corresponding

blank(s) (e.g., _ _ _ m_ _ _ _). If the word or phrase does not contain the letter, then one element of the hangman's gallows is drawn.
4. Completing a character in a noose requires a minimum of six wrong answers.
5. The first player to guess the word or phrase wins the game and is the recorder (in this case, the person who draws the hangman) for the next round.

❧ WORD ASSOCIATION

From a list of words, associate pairs of words that might belong together. For example, for the list *novice, virtuoso, accomplice, kindergartner, crook,* one association would be *kindergartner–novice.* To further enrich vocabulary, have each participant explain the connection between the words. Associations can be created by thinking of words that mean the same thing (synonyms) or words that mean the opposite of each other (antonyms). This skill not only helps build oral vocabulary, but it helps make written language more colorful through the use of powerful descriptive words or adjectives.

❧ ATTRIBUTE WORDS

1. Write attribute words on index cards (e.g., coarse, smooth, glowing, horrific, terrific, amazing).
2. Divide the group into two teams.
3. The teams take turns pulling an attribute card, with each team member suggesting something the word could describe.
4. If each team member can produce a word, the team earns a point.

Acronyms and Initialisms

Another effective means to build vocabulary is to work with acronyms and initialisms. Acronyms are abbreviations formed from the first letters of a word or phrase and are pronounced as if they are words (e.g., NASA, SONAR). Initialisms are made from the first letter of a string of words but cannot be pronounced as words themselves (e.g., FBI, CIA).

❧ Word Games

Play various word games, such as Bingo or Scrabble, using acronyms and initialisms. In Bingo, the objective of the game would be to provide the definition and match it with the appropriate acronym. In Scrabble, the player would use letters to spell various acronyms, instead of spelling words. Another activity is to provide letters and challenge participants to come up with the correct acronym. See the following list of acronyms and initialisms. Encourage participants to think of others.

ASAP: As soon as possible; used when encouraging someone to respond to a request without delay.

BYOB: Bring your own bottle; used for party invitations that advise guests that limited beverages are to be provided and guests are encouraged to bring their own.

ESL: English as a second language.

FBI: Federal Bureau of Investigation.

FHA: Federal Housing Administration; created to help people secure loans to buy houses.

PS: Postscript; people sometimes include PS at the end of a letter to include additional thoughts that were meant to be included in the body of the letter but were forgotten.

RSVP: *Répondez s'il vous plaît,* French for "Please reply." This acronym often is used on invitations to parties and other special events.

SSA: Social Security Administration; the Social Security Act created a national pension for retired people, as well as unemployment insurance.

UNICEF: United Nations Children's Fund.

Written Language

The written language activities and lessons that follow incorporate many styles of writing, including expository, descriptive, persuasive, and narrative. Also included are lessons on writing folklore and poetry. The lessons help to develop and strengthen writing skills through planning, revising, editing, and rewriting targeted elements—for example, by adding descriptive words and phrases. Participants will enrich their vocabulary and sharpen their critical-thinking skills as they work to sequence events and ideas, strengthen their word choice and sentence patterns, and develop characters and mood.

Activities

Following is a list of fun written language activities—warm-up and longer—to supplement the lessons.

- Write reviews for novels.
- Make up a questionnaire to review a book.
- Read a mystery and make predictions along the way.
- Create a mystery scenario. Have participants role-play or record facts to solve the mystery.
- Change the ending of a novel.
- Change a novel into a play and perform it.
- Create a comic strip, or white-out the words in a comic strip and add new words.
- Write jokes.
- Analyze a piece of artwork.

❧ Read and analyze poetry.

❧ Create posters for events.

❧ Describe the seasons, listing nouns, verbs, and adjectives. For example:

Winter
Nouns: snow, hot chocolate, jackets, scarves, sleds
Adjectives: cold, windy, icy, snowy, freezing
Verbs: skate, ski, freeze

Spring
Nouns: flowers, butterflies, bunnies, raindrops
Adjectives: green, fresh, colorful, cheerful
Verbs: rain, grow, clean, drizzle

Summer
Nouns: beach, pool, sun
Adjectives: hot, bright, sunny, humid
Verbs: sweat, swim, surf

Fall
Nouns: leaves, rake, pumpkin, acorns
Adjectives: cloudy, orange, colorful
Verbs: harvest, pick, trick or treat

❧ Write about a favorite season, then illustrate the season using a variety of media (e.g., collage, watercolors, crayon resist, oil pastels).

❧ Bring in words to research; create word searches and crossword puzzles.

❧ Gather the group to do crossword puzzles.

❧ Share poetry. Invite the group to share their favorite poems that contain figurative language (language that uses figures of speech—such as metaphors and similes—to go beyond the literal meanings of the words; see "Figurative Language" in the Glossary).

❧ Write a figure of speech about how you'd feel after these events:

Winning a gold medal in the Olympics
Graduating
Celebrating a birthday
Losing a competition

- Write a simile that describes your feeling when eating popcorn, pizza, ice cream, or chocolate cake.
- Write a metaphor that expresses your feeling on a gloomy day, windy day, rainy day, or sunny day.
- Write a personification about how your house might feel every time you leave or what your bed feels every time you jump in it.
- Write an advertisement for your community.
- Given a short story or article to read, make a list of 10 descriptive words. Use 5 of them in a sentence. Challenge the group to use the other 5 in a sentence.
- Write a paragraph about a character from a book or short story that you either liked or disliked. Give reasons for your choice.
- Make up a new title for a book or story. Explain why you like the new title.
- What would you do if you were king or queen for a day?
- What would you ask for if a fairy gave you three wishes?
- A talking horse comes to your bedroom. What would you say to him?
- You are riding on a merry-go-round. Suddenly it stops and your horse runs away. What would you do?
- Suppose you could talk to animals. Which animal would be your best friend? What would you talk about?
- Use your imagination. What might happen if these things changed?

> Your life span increased by 50 years.
> The government paid all of your expenses required to remain independent.
> You were young again.

- Have you ever heard these expressions: "Sharp as a tack" or "Fit as a fiddle"? These are similes. Fill in the blanks in the phrases below. Try to create original expressions.

As funny as _____.	As loud as _____.
As nervous as _____.	As wet as _____.
As hard as _____.	As quiet as _____.
As smart as _____.	As cool as _____.
As crooked as _____.	As bright as _____.

❧ When you see a peacock or read about one, feathers, beauty, and color might come to mind. What ideas come to mind when you think of these things?

Soul music	A pond
A snow-capped mountain	Champagne
A large shady tree	A record player
A honeybee	The seasons
Hot chocolate	Tennis shoes

❧ Would you go on a camping trip or a trip to the moon? Why? What would you do?

❧ What would you do if you were lost in the woods? Describe your feelings.

❧ Before you begin to read a novel or short story, first write a summary of what the title makes you think of. After you have read the book, compare and contrast your account of the novel or story to what you read.

❧ Play word games using idioms. An idiom is an expression or a phrase composed of two or more words and is a figure of speech. The expression is not interpreted literally, but rather is understood to mean something quite different from what specific words of the phrase imply. A few idioms are listed below; additional idioms are provided in appendix A.

"Like a chicken with its head cut off" (in a wild and crazy manner)
"Till the cows come home" (for a long time)
"Fat cat" (a person with a lot of money and importance)
"Blind as a bat" (unaware)
"Duck soup" (something easily done with no problems)
"Frog in one's throat" (a hoarse voice)
"From the horse's mouth" (from someone who knows what he or she is talking about)

❧ Make up spelling games. For example, Don't Misspell "Misspell." Make double-sided cards, one side with the correct spelling of a word and the other with the incorrect spelling. Following is a list of some commonly misspelled words. (For additional commonly misspelled words, see appendix A.)

category–catergory	neighbor–neighbore
embarrass–embarass	noticeable–noticable
existence–existance	pastime–passtime
grateful–greatful	relevant–relevent
license–lisence	restaurant–restarant
misspell–mispell	tomorrow–tommorrow

❧ Create a mnemonic device. Explain that the mother of the Muses was named Mnemosyne. She was the goddess of memory. We use a form of her name to refer to memory; for example, a mnemonic device is a trick that triggers memory. Think of tricks you can use to remember difficult vocabulary words. Work with a partner.

❧ Read a well-known fairy tale and rewrite it from the villain's point of view. For example, rewrite the story of the "Three Little Pigs" from the wolf's point of view. A good example of this is *The True Story of the Three Little Pigs* by Jon Scieszka and Lane Smith.

❧ Research the history and country for food words. See the sample list below. (For additional food words, see appendix A.)

> *Avocado:* Originated from the Aztec of Mexico, by way of Spanish explorers. Spanish explorers returned from Mexico with avocados. They are sometimes referred to as "alligator pears."
> *Banana:* Originated from Africa, by way of European explorers.
> *Bologna:* Named after the Italian city of Bologna.
> *Coffee:* Turkish, based on the name of the area in Ethiopia (Kaff), where the plant grows.

❧ Bring in menus from different types of restaurants. Look through them and choose words to research. Share recipes from various cultures and why you like them. Present a brief talk on recipe ingredients and preparation. Suggestions are provided below. (See "Listening Activities and Lessons" and appendix A for additional recipes.)

❧ Salsa-Vocado

Ingredients list for each participant

½ cup salsa

2 avocados

1 tablespoon lime juice

1 tablespoon chopped cilantro

Salt

Tortilla chips

Directions

1. Remove the pit from both avocados, spoon out the meat, and mash with a fork.
2. In a bowl, mix salsa with mashed avocado.
3. Add lime juice and cilantro to mixture.
4. Add salt to taste.
5. Serve with tortilla chips.

❧ Tortellini Kebabs

Ingredients list for each participant

1 cup cooked tortellini

1 cup cherry tomatoes

½ block mozzarella cheese

Olive oil or pesto

Salt and pepper

Directions

1. Cut mozzarella cheese into 1-inch cubes.
2. Toss cooked tortellini, tomatoes, and cheese blocks in olive oil or pesto.
3. Add salt and pepper to taste.
4. Thread tortellini, cheese, and tomatoes on skewers.

Lessons and Steps
for Various Writing Styles
EXPOSITORY WRITING

Expository writing is used to explain, describe, give information, or inform. This type of writing frequently is used when presenting reports or writing essays. The text is organized around one topic and developed according to a pattern.

One expository pattern is describing a topic by listing characteristics, features, and examples, providing details about how something looks, feels, tastes, smells, sounds, or makes one feel. It can also include sequencing, in which the author lists items or events in numerical or chronological order. Cue words include *first, second, third, next, then,* and *finally.*

Another pattern is comparing and contrasting. A comparison essay usually discusses the similarities between two things, whereas a contrast essay discusses the differences.

An author can focus on the relationship between two or more events or experiences and develop a cause-and-effect essay. This pattern could address both cause and effect or simply discuss one or the other.

Another pattern is problem-solution writing. In this type of essay, the author states a problem and lists one or more solutions.

Expository essays are written to demonstrate knowledge and understanding of a topic. The writer cannot assume that the reader or listener has prior knowledge or understanding of the topic. To reinforce clarity, one of the most important mechanisms for developing expository skills is to improve the organization of the text.

WRITING AN EXPOSITORY ESSAY

Choose a topic, such as how technology has changed the lives of seniors. Write an introductory paragraph containing the thesis (main idea). In the next three paragraphs, provide details to support the thesis. In the last paragraph, restate the thesis and tie together the major points of the essay.

Steps for Writing an Expository Essay

1. *Prewriting:* Brainstorm the topic or main idea.
   - Research and take notes on the topic.
   - Create an outline of the information to be presented in each paragraph.
   - Organize the information in a logical sequence.
2. *Drafting:* Write a rough draft.
   - In the first paragraph, state the thesis clearly without giving an opinion or taking a position.
   - In the next three paragraphs, cover points that develop the thesis. The closing sentence in each of the paragraphs should offer facts and examples in support of the paragraph's topic.
   - In the concluding paragraph, reinforce the thesis and main supporting ideas.
   - Write the essay in third-person voice (he, she, or it). Avoid the words *I* and *you.*
3. *Revising:* Review, modify, and reorganize.
   - Is the information clearly and effectively communicated to the reader?
   - Does the essay convey an unbiased analysis of relevant facts that unfolds logically?
   - Is the sentence structure and word choice varied?
   - Does it include transitions between sentences and paragraphs to help the reader's understanding?
   - Does the concluding paragraph communicate the meaning and importance of the thesis and key supporting ideas?
4. *Editing:* Proofread and correct errors in grammar and mechanics. Improve clarity and style.
5. *Publishing:* Prepare a final copy and share with the group.

DESCRIPTIVE WRITING

A descriptive essay describes something (e.g., an object, a person, a place, an experience, an emotion, or a situation). It paints a vivid picture in the reader's mind and appeals to the senses through the process of describing how some-thing looks, sounds, feels, smells, and tastes.

❧ WRITING A DESCRIPTIVE ESSAY
Steps for Writing a Descriptive Essay
1. *Select a subject:* Make detailed observation notes on your subject. If it is a place, try to visit and record how it looks, sounds, and smells. Appeal to the senses. Take time to brainstorm; for example, if you are describing your favorite food, choose words that are connected to the food (for instance, pizza: sauce, cheese, crust, pepperoni spices, steaming, melted). After making a list, begin compiling descriptive lists for each word. Consider this: If the reader begins craving the pizza, the goal of the essay has been achieved.
2. *Select pertinent details:* Choose words carefully; use clear and concise language.
3. *Organize the details:* Think about the structure of the paragraphs. For example, are they written chronologically (in time order) or from general to specific? Will the structure make sense to the reader?
4. *Use vivid language:* Avoid using vague words or generalities—such as good, nice, bad, or smart. Be specific and use descriptive words (for example, note the difference between "My class is smart" and "My class is a sea of knowledge"). Provide sensory details such as those listed below.
   - Smells ("The aroma of the freshly baked cookies made my mouth water.")
   - Sounds ("The sounds of bells and of children playing at school make me happy.")
   - Sights ("The sunset wrapped around the mountain like a halo on the horizon.")
   - Taste ("My eyes popped and started to water as I bit into the hot chili pepper.")
   - Touch ("The pillow was as soft as a plump marshmallow.")
5. *Draw a logical conclusion:* The conclusion also can use descriptive words, but make sure they are relevant.

Persuasive Writing

In persuasive writing, the writer takes a position for or against an issue and writes to convince others to agree with the facts presented and the opinion shared. Persuasive or argumentative essays use logic and reason to show that one idea is more legitimate than another idea. The argument should be based on sound reasoning and solid evidence. Elements toward building a good persuasive essay include establishing facts to support the argument, classifying relevant values for the audience, prioritizing, editing, and sequencing the facts, and forming and stating conclusions.

❧ Writing a Persuasive Essay

Important points to remember:

- Choose an issue or problem and decide which position to take and to write about. Also think about the solution.
- Research the topic. Try to think beyond personal experience or knowledge and instead refer to experts on the topic.
- Make sure the topic of thesis has two sides; it must be debatable.
- Disprove the opposing argument.
- Take a stance and support it with evidence.

Steps for Writing a Persuasive Essay

1. *Introduction:* Introduce the topic and tell the reader the point of view of the essay. Think of opening statements that grab the reader (e.g., open with a quotation, an anecdote, a statistic or fact, a question, or an exaggeration or outrageous statement). Next state the thesis or purpose of the essay. This should serve as the foundation and guide to writing the essay.
2. *Body:* The body of the essay justifies and provides evidence to support the opinion in the thesis statement. The writer should attempt to anticipate opposing viewpoints and provide counterarguments along with the main points of the essay. Examples to support a persuasive essay include the following.

- *Facts:* Record facts from reading, observation, or personal experience. Facts can be proven.
- *Statistics:* Make sure the data come from responsible sources and cite the sources.
- *Quotes:* Research direct quotes from leading experts to use to support the position put forth in the essay.

3. *Conclusion:* Restate the thesis or focus statement and summarize the main points. Think of a personal comment that can be expressed through a question, a quotation, or by making a prediction or recommendation.

⚜ WRITING AN ADVERTISEMENT

Participants use a print or television advertisement as a guide for designing their own advertisement for a product to enhance their community.

Guided Practice: Write a Critique

1. Identify the strengths and weaknesses of the advertisement. What are the strongest and weakest components of its persuasive argument?
2. Make a list of persuasive words.
3. Identify the targeted audience.
4. Define the main message the writer wants the audience to know about the product.
5. Determine the tone (e.g., funny, silly, serious, or informative).

Independent Activity: Create Your Own Advertisement

Create an advertisement to enhance your community. Make sure all of the elements of a persuasive essay are included.

1. Decide what to persuade others to do or think and determine how to accomplish the task.
2. Keep the target audience in mind. Who will buy the product? What are its benefits? List its pros and cons.
3. Create a product name. Determine the purpose of the product and what it will do.
4. Decide on a message that will capture the audience. Think about visuals to help get the message across.

5. Make up a slogan for the ad, choosing words wisely. Use words that produce positive feelings, such as *happiness, joy, warmth, beauty, dazzling,* and *amazing.* Be aware that using the wrong words can generate negative feelings. Different words work for different audiences.

NARRATIVE WRITING

Narrative writing most often tells a story. It relates a clear sequence of events that occurs over time. These essays often are anecdotal, experiential, and personal and allow writers to be creative and moving in their expression. If written as a story, a narrative essay should include the conventions of storytelling such as plot, character, setting, climax, and ending. It should be filled with details that are carefully selected to explain, support, and embellish the story.

In some cases, a narrative essay is not written as a story (a book report, for example). Narrative writing focuses on providing an informative account for the reader. It should make a point and have a purpose. A good narrative includes many of the elements common to most styles of writing. See the following guidelines for producing a strong narrative writing piece.

❧ WRITING A NARRATIVE ESSAY

Describe the setting by using colors, smells, and sounds—use all five senses. Describe how something feels, tastes, looks, and smells. Research the setting to accurately describe the animals, trees, plants, and flowers indigenous to the area. Plan the timing and sequence of events. Add details throughout to sustain the interest of the reader.

Have the characters express their feelings instead of simply stating what they can do or want to do. For example, "I went to the mall on a rainy day" is much more descriptive when expressed as "I splashed across the parking lot, dripping wet, and barely made it into the mall before lightning struck."

Steps for Writing a Narrative Essay

1. Develop the characters. Write descriptions of physical features; include personality characteristics.

2. Decide what message to convey to the reader, such as working together or helping others.

3. Develop the plot:
   - Make the beginning interesting.
   - Create a conflict or question requiring resolution.
   - Produce an ending that completes the story. Ending techniques can describe a character's memories, decisions, actions, feelings, hopes, and wishes as a result of the events in the story. Examples:

     Memory: I will never forget the time. . . .

     Feeling: I can still feel the. . . .

     Hope or wish: I hope that the time I. . . .

     Decision: From that day on, I decided to. . . .

4. Ask questions:
   - Does it make sense?
   - Does it flow well?
   - Is the story interesting?
   - Does it have a hook or phrase to make it memorable?

5. Consider content and organization:
   - Is the topic paragraph developed fully through the use of examples?
   - Does each sentence in a paragraph relate to the topic sentence?
   - Are the ideas presented in a reasonable order?
   - Are transitional words and phrases used and written between paragraphs? (Instead of saying "next" and "then," say "suddenly," "all of a sudden," or "a moment later.")

6. Rewrite many times. Rewriting is a way of going deeper into the story.

❧ WRITING A MYSTERY: IDEAS FOR GETTING STARTED

Participants develop a mystery scenario starring themselves as the main character.

Steps for Writing a Mystery

1. Choose and describe the setting.
   - What do you see? (A shadow in the bushes; a silhouette in the mirror?)
   - What do you hear? (Footsteps on the stairs; heavy breathing on the phone; a creaking floor?)
   - What do you smell? (The scent of a stale cigar creeping in the room?)

- What do you feel? (A chill through an open window; a draft from an open door?)
2. Consider: What mysterious event happens to make the story suspenseful? (Maybe the door mysteriously opens as you notice a shadow in the window.)
3. Build up tension to make the story intriguing.
   - Create pitfalls for the main character (you) to encounter.
   - Think about weaknesses or fears the main character may have.
   - Develop strange and unforeseen events.
   - Think of dangerous predicaments the main character could get into.
4. Include thrilling cliff-hangers to keep the reader intrigued. For example:
   - You fall in a snake pit.
   - You are surrounded by a pack of wolves.
   - You are in a dilemma and have to make a life-changing decision.
5. The resolution of the mystery should provide a fulfilling conclusion. For example:
   - The main character (you) becomes a hero.
   - A surprising twist is revealed at the end.
6. After writing your mystery, read all but the ending to a partner and challenge him or her to solve it.

Deconstructing a Narrative

Given a short narrative story, participants take apart the story by answering questions specific to a narrative writing.

Directed Instruction
1. Activate prior knowledge: Ask the group to describe narrative writing.
2. Read a selected short story individually or as a group.
3. Ask the group what makes this story a narrative.
4. Create a storyboard (see appendix C for a template), illustrating the setting (when and where), characters (main and supporting), and parts of a narrative plot (exposition, rising action, climax, falling action, and resolution).
5. Complete the storyboard as a group.

6. Brainstorm ideas about what makes the story interesting.
7. *Option:* Draw a picture that represents the main idea of the story.

❧ INTERVIEWING AN OLDER PERSON

Match up students with older adults to conduct an interview. After an initial visit, students write a narrative about their older adult partner. In order to build relationships, this activity takes place over time.

Directed Instruction
1. Have the group come up with a list of questions for students to ask. Sample questions:
   - How has the world changed since you were a student?
   - What is the most important lesson you've learned in your life?
   - What significant advice would you give to your grandchildren or to students?
   - What was the happiest time in your life?
   - How did you entertain yourself as a child?
   - How has technology changed since you were a child? What surprises you the most?
2. Discuss the questions and determine which ones will generate the most interesting responses.
3. Narrow down the questions and create a questionnaire. (See appendix C for sample questionnaires.)
4. Encourage the students to take good notes.
5. The students write their interview as a narrative, including vivid details and humor when possible.
6. The students share their writing with the person interviewed before presenting the narrative to the group.

As a variation, reverse the lesson and have the older person interview his or her student partner.

FOLKLORE

For the purposes of this curriculum, folklore refers to the traditional beliefs, myths, tales, and practices of a group of people that have traditionally been handed down orally. Myths and folktales are types of folklore.

Below are some different aspects of folklore.

Behavioral Lore: Family and local customs and celebrations. For example, the practice of throwing rice at a wedding for good luck, or jumping the broom to complete a wedding ceremony.

Children's Lore: Games that children play, such as jacks, hide-and-seek, hopscotch, jump rope chants, and marbles. Sayings such as "Step on a crack, break your mother's back." Telling ghost stories around a campfire.

Community Lore: One aspect of community lore is how a community celebrates holidays. For example, are there parades? Are Chinese New Year or Cinco de Mayo celebrated?

Family Lore: Many families have their own stories, passed down from generation to generation. Stories about grandparents, aunts, uncles, cousins, and other relatives passed on and remembered—all are part of a person's family folklore.

Material Items: Musical instruments, clothing, jewelry, quilts, home decorations, puppets, foods (including special recipes) all can be handed down.

Oral Traditions: These include songs, lullabies, poetry, jokes, riddles, proverbs, special sayings, myths, and folktales.

The web resources list at the end of this book contains a link to a good source for folklore.

❧ WRITING ABOUT FOLKLORE
1. As a group, brainstorm different types of folklore.
2. Discuss the kinds of folklore personally experienced.
3. Have participants share with a partner their most memorable tradition from childhood.
4. As a group, create a collection of community or family lore.

5. Have participants choose one community or family lore to research, asking the following questions:
   - How did the event get started?
   - How long has it been going on?
   - Does it vary from country to country? If so, describe how.
6. Participants write a folklore of their own.

Myths

Myths are often ancient stories about supernatural entities. The purpose of these types of myths is to provide a unique explanation for natural phenomena, such as where thunder comes from, or how the sun got into the sky.

❧ WRITING A MYTH

1. Choose a natural phenomenon to write about. Select something that is familiar that can be observed. For example:
   - If you live in California, explain why the ground shakes during an earthquake.
   - If you live on the East Coast, explain how snow can cover the ground like an icy blanket.
   - If you live in the Midwest, explain how the twists and turns of a tornado can snap up a whole house within seconds.
2. Research the chosen phenomenon.
   - Take notes about the smells, sights, and sounds connected to it. Think of yourself as a reporter.
   - Think of key words that describe the phenomenon and look for descriptive synonyms.
   - Brainstorm a variety of scenarios that could happen. Think in terms of what if?
   - Try working with a partner to come up with ideas.

Folktales

Folktales often illustrate the magic of clever animals that take on human characteristics. Most folktales convey a message or moral.

❧ Writing a Folktale

1. Choose a topic you've wondered about or something that interests you. For example:
   - How elephants got long trunks.
   - Why penguins can't fly.
   - Why giraffes have long necks.
2. As a group, brainstorm story morals.
3. Try to use at least two animals that represent opposing qualities. This helps to set up the conflict or problem within the story.

Poetry

Poetry is a literary work in which special intensity is given to the expression of feelings and ideas by use of distinctive style and rhythm. But what is poetry, really? Like love, poetry is difficult to define, and it can be expressed in many ways and forms. William Wordsworth defined poetry as "the spontaneous overflow of powerful feelings." Edgar Allan Poe said that poetry is "the rhythmical creation of beauty in words." And in his article "What Is Poetry?" contemporary literature expert Mark Flanagan says this: "[Poetry] typically evokes in the reader intense emotion: joy, sorrow, anger, catharsis, love. . . Alternatively, poetry has the ability to surprise the reader with an Ah Ha! Experience — revelation, insight, further understanding of elemental truth and beauty. . . . Poetry is imagination" ("What is poetry? An Introduction," https://www.thoughtco.com/what-is-poetry-852737).

Poetry, therefore, means different things to different people. The objective here is to identify and write poetry in its many forms and styles that have evolved over the centuries, starting with one of the simplest and most familiar forms: the acrostic poem.

Acrostic

An acrostic is a poem in which the first letter of each line spells out a word or phrase. Usually the first letter of each line is capitalized so that the word or phrase spelled out is easy to recognize. Acrostic poems tend to be easy to write because they do not have to rhyme or have rhythm, and there is also no limit on how long or short a line needs to be. Additionally, an acrostic can be used as a mnemonic device to aid memory retrieval. Below are the steps for writing an acrostic poem.

1. Decide on a subject word or phrase for the poem.
2. Write the subject vertically on the page.
3. Think about words or phrases that describe the subject that start with a letter in the subject name.
4. Continue filling in the rest of the lines to create a poem.
5. The lines should relate to one other.
6. The poem should make sense. For example, "dad":

Dependable
And
Delightful

❧ WRITING AN ACROSTIC
Participants write an acrostic poem using a person's name.

Directed Instruction
1. As a group, brainstorm adjectives that could describe a person. Think of at least one adjective for each letter of the alphabet and create a list.
2. Have participants write their names vertically on a paper plate.
3. Participants then circulate and ask others to add a descriptive adjective for a letter of their name. For example, if a person's name has five letters, then he or she would approach five different people to supply an adjective.

Independent Activity
1. Choose a name for the person you would like to write about.
2. Think of a message you would like to convey to that person.
3. Use a thesaurus (if available) to find words to describe that person.
4. Write the person's name vertically on a piece of paper.
5. Add a descriptive adjective for each letter of the name.

Extended Activity
Create a card to write the message in. Make it seasonal if possible.

Ballad

A ballad is a simple narrative poem that tells a story. It is a way for the poet to share any heartfelt experience and is often used in songs. The first line of a ballad is the most important because it introduces the story. The poet may choose the rhyme scheme—the pattern of rhyme that comes at the end of each verse.

The most common rhyme scheme is AAB: four stanzas (groups) of three lines in which the first two lines rhyme (AA) and the third line is different (B). This type of poem is unique because it includes choruses. Typically, the third line of each stanza is the chorus. The chorus should be something that is relevant throughout the poem, because it is repeated several times.

Other common rhyme schemes are ABCB (lines 2 and 4 rhyme) and ABAB (lines 1 and 3 rhyme; lines 2 and 4 rhyme). In these schemes, the first and third lines have four beats and the second and fourth lines have three beats.

The web resources list toward the back of this book contains a link to a good source for ballads.

❧ WRITING A BALLAD

After listening to or reading several ballads, participants write a ballad using rhythm and narrative structure.

Directed Instruction
1. Review the characteristics of a ballad:
   - It has rhythm, rhyme, and repetition.
   - It contains some dialogue within the poem.
   - It uses a rhyme scheme. Common rhyme schemes are AAB (lines 1 and 2 rhyme), ABCB (lines 2 and 4 rhyme), and ABAB (lines 1 and 3 rhyme; lines 2 and 4 rhyme).
   - It tells a story.
2. Read a ballad to the group and ask them to listen for the rhythm.

3. Identify and write out the rhythm of the lines in each stanza.
4. Discuss the story told in the ballad.

Independent Activity
Have participants write a ballad of their own.

Cinquain

Cinquains are five lines long with only a few words on each line, which makes them fairly easy to write. The first and last lines have two syllables. The middle lines have more syllables—which makes the shape of the lines of the poem into a diamond, similar to the poetic form called the *diamante*. Typically, the second line has four syllables, the third line has six syllables, and the fourth line has eight syllables.

Cinquains do not have to rhyme, but they can consist of rhymes. Even though they are just five lines long, the best cinquains tell a story. Instead of just using descriptive words, cinquains can have an action (something happening), a feeling caused by the action, and a conclusion or ending. Following are three formats for cinquains.

Format 1

Line 1:	One word	Seniors
Line 2:	Two words	Lived well
Line 3:	Three words	Through changing seasons
Line 4:	Four words	Building beautiful and memorable
Line 5:	One word	Legacies

Format 2

Line 1:	A noun	Kittens
Line 2:	Two adjectives	Cuddly, furry
Line 3:	Three " -ing" words	Purring, prancing, leaping
Line 4:	A phrase	Into a tangled ball of yarn
Line 5:	Another word for the noun	Playful

Format 3

Line 1:	Two syllables	Winning!
Line 2:	Four syllables	What is the game?
Line 3:	Six syllables	The number is sixteen
Line 4:	Eight syllables	Diagonal, one space to go
Line 5:	Two syllables	Bingo!

WRITING A CINQUAIN

Participants write a cinquain following a simple model.

Directed Instruction

1. Introduce the group to a variety of cinquains. (The web resources list toward the back of this book contains a link to a good source for cinquains.)
2. Choose a subject to write about as a group, such as:
   - Favorite things
   - Things you dislike
   - Something you see around you
   - Something that happens to you
3. Brainstorm words or phrases associated with the subject.
4. Think about the story you want to convey to the reader.
5. Write the words and phrases in an order that tells the story.

   Here's an example of a cinquain about Jell-O that follows format 3.

Jell-O

Cold and yummy

It wiggles and it shakes

As it flows through the hungry child's

Tummy

Independent Practice

Create a cinquain using the model given below.

Title _____

Subject _____

Description _____, _____,
Action (" -ing" words) _____, _____, _____,
Feeling _____
Conclusion _____

Diamante

Diamante is the Italian word for "diamond," and this poetic form, created in 1969 by American poet Iris McClellan Tiedt, is named for its diamond shape. The text is composed of seven lines. Each line uses specific types of words, such as adjectives and " -ing" words. This type of poem does not have to rhyme. There are two different types of diamantes: the synonym diamante and antonym diamante. Following are the guidelines for writing a diamante:

Seven lines long. The first and last lines contain just one word.
The second and sixth lines contain two words.
The third and fifth lines contain three words.
The fourth line contains four words.
Lines one, four, and seven contain nouns.
Lines two and six contain adjectives.
Lines three and five contain verbs.

Noun
Adjective, Adjective
Verb, Verb, Verb
Noun, Noun, Noun, Noun
Verb, Verb, Verb
Adjective, Adjective
Noun

In a synonym diamante, the nouns are at the beginning and end. The nouns should be two words that have basically the same meaning (are synonyms).

Clowns
Funny, Silly
Laughing, Joking, Chuckling
Actors, Jesters, Comedians, Buffoons
Smiling, Mocking, Giggling
Zany, Happy
Comics

In the synonym diamante provided, the words *clowns* and *comics* are synonyms. In an antonym diamante, the two nouns are opposites. In the antonym diamante below, turtles and rabbits are positioned as opposites.

Turtles
Sleepy, Calm
Hiding, Swimming, Crawling
Shells, Reptiles, Fur, Mammals
Hopping, Nibbling, Darting
Alert, Quick
Rabbits

❧ WRITING A DIAMANTE

Following the diamante format, participants create a synonym and an antonym diamante.

1. Choose two subjects to write about; the subjects selected must be nouns.
2. Next, brainstorm adjectives and verbs that describe the two nouns. Use columns to list the subjects and the adjectives that describe them, as shown in the example below:

Cats	Dogs
Quiet	Playful
Gentle	Wild
Purring	Barking
Scratching	Fetching
Climbing	Digging

3. Arrange the poem like this:
- Place the subjects (either synonyms or antonyms) at the top and bottom (lines 1 and 7)
- Place the adjectives on lines 2 and 6.
- Place the verbs on lines 3 and 5.
- Finally, place the additional nouns on line 4. The first two nouns should relate to the subject on line 1; the last two nouns should relate to the subject on line 7.

Cats

quiet, gentle

purring, scratching, climbing

claws, milk, paws, bones

barking, fetching, digging

playful, wild

Dogs

4. Once complete, share the poems with the group.

Haiku

Haiku are short poems that use sensory language to capture an image. They are often inspired by an element of nature, a twinkling of beauty, or an amazing experience. Noticing something that makes you say *Look at that!* is the perfect stimulus for writing a haiku.

Typically, a haiku is a three-line poem with a 5-7-5 pattern (5 syllables, 7 syllables, 5 syllables). Over time this pattern has been broken, but the philosophy of the haiku has been preserved. The power of this style of poetry lies in its brevity. As noted, it focuses on a brief moment in time (like taking a snapshot of something, such as a frog jumping onto a lily pad or rain falling onto a leaf). How would someone describe these images in a way that projects the experience to the reader? In other words, instead of saying how a scene makes one feel, the poet shows the details that caused the emotion.

Originally created by Japanese poets, haiku must contain a *kigo,* or season word. For example, cherry blossoms indicate spring and snowcapped mountains indicate winter. An activity to spark the writing of a haiku poem is showing photos as a prompt. Begin by displaying photos that illustrate the wonders of nature.

Following are some examples of haiku poetry. It is the beauty and simplicity of the haiku form that inspires poets.

> White caps on the bay:
> A broken signboard banging
> In the April wind.
> ("White Caps on the Bay" from *Haiku: This Other World*
>   by Richard Wright)

> Spring is in the air
> Flowers are blooming sky high
> Children are laughing
> ("Spring Is in the Air" by Kaitlyn Guenther)[1]

> Sand scatters the beach
> Waves crash on the sandy shore
> Blue water shimmers
> ("Beaches" by Kaitlyn Guenther)[2]

Writing a Haiku
Participants write a haiku inspired by nature.

Directed Instruction
1. As a group, read a variety of haiku poems about nature. (The web resources list at the end of this book contains a link to a good source for haiku poetry.)
2. Review the characteristics of haiku.
3. Take a nature walk and tune into the surroundings. Have participants carry a notebook and write down lines that come to them.

---

[1] "Spring Is in the Air" reprinted with permission from http://www.dltk-kids.com/.

[2] "Beaches" reprinted with permission from http://www.dltk-kids.com/.

4. Ask these questions: Which details in the environment spark an interest? What makes them stand out?
5. For the first haiku, participants should adhere to the 5-7-5 pattern. After mastering the writing of a haiku, they may branch out and use other patterns.
6. Share haikus with the group.

Extended Activities

- Choose haiku poems from the group to analyze. Here is an example using one of my haikus, "The Ocean."

   How many syllables are in each line?
       Tides roll in and out (___ syllables)
       Sea creatures crawl in silence (___ syllables)
       While waves crash afar (___ syllables)
   Name and describe the subject of the haiku: _____

- Play a riddle game with haiku poems. Ask: What am I?

Limerick

Limerick poems were popularized by Edward Lear, an English poet who in 1846 published the *Book of Nonsense*. A limerick is a five-line witty poem with a distinctive rhythm. Limericks are fun to write because they are short, they rhyme, they are funny, and they have a bouncy rhythm that makes them easy to memorize. The syllable count for limericks is shown here:

Line 1: 7 to 10 syllables
Line 2: 7 to 10 syllables
Line 3: 5 to 7 syllables
Line 4: 5 to 7 syllables
Line 5: 7 to 10 syllables

The rhyme scheme is AABBA (lines 1, 2, and 5 rhyme; lines 3 and 4 rhyme).

The following is a well-known limerick. The underlines indicate the syllables to stress.

> There <u>was</u> an old <u>man</u> from Nan<u>tuck</u>et,
> Who <u>kept</u> all his <u>cash</u> in a <u>buck</u>et.
> His <u>daugh</u>ter, named <u>Nan</u>,
> Ran a<u>way</u> with a <u>man</u>,
> And <u>as</u> for the <u>buck</u>et, Nan<u>tuck</u>et.

Try clapping the following rhythm while reciting the limerick about Hall below:

> clap CLAP clap clap CLAP clap clap CLAP
> clap CLAP clap clap CLAP clap clap CLAP
> clap clap CLAP clap clap CLAP
> clap clap CLAP clap clap CLAP
> clap clap CLAP clap clap CLAP clap clap CLAP

> There <u>was</u> a young <u>fel</u>low named <u>Hall</u>,
> Who <u>fell</u> in the <u>spring</u> in the <u>fall</u>.
> 'Twould have <u>been</u> a sad <u>thing</u>,
> Had he <u>died</u> in the <u>spring</u>.
> But he <u>did</u>n't—he <u>died</u> in the <u>fall</u>.

With limericks, generally the first line ends with the name of a person or place and the last line is funny.

⁂ WRITING A LIMERICK
Participants write a limerick incorporating the names of unknown people.
1. Go on excursions that enable the group to people-watch and imagine what other people's lives might be like.
2. Build on a name: Check the visitor's list in your facility, or use the names of administrators. Form a mental picture of the person.
3. Develop a questionnaire: Discuss dreams, fears, family (e.g., married, children, grandchildren).

4. Present a problem: How will the character react?
5. Break it down further:
   - Think of a strong emotion.
   - Write a list of situations that could inspire that emotion.
   - Come up with a variety of scenarios for each situation. For example: What if you won a million dollars?
   - State what caused the situation.

Couplet

Couplets consist of a pair of successive rhyming lines, usually of the same length, that make up a complete thought. They can be as short as one couplet (two lines), or as long as it takes to tell the story. The shorter the poem, the more impact each word should have.

Couplets can be formal (closed) or run-on (open). In formal couplets, there is a grammatical pause at the end of each verse (line). In a run-on (or open) couplet, the meaning of the first verse continues into the second.

The rhyme scheme in couplets is the simplest in poetry. The rhyme tends to call attention to itself. Writing couplets is an easy way to start writing poetry. Below is an example of a couplet:

> Working together is the way
> To make learning fun today
> Those who are caring
> Will always enjoy sharing
> So before the day is done
> Learning should be fun

Concrete (Shape)

Concrete poetry, or shape poetry, is a style of poetry in which the visual appearance matches the topic of the poem. The words form shapes that illustrate a poem's subject, as well as its literal meaning. For example, if the subject of the poem is a flower, the poem is shaped like a flower. This form of poetry has been in use for more than 2,000 years, as far back as the third century BCE in Greece.

✣ WRITING A CONCRETE POEM

Participants choose a subject and write a concrete poem.

1. Choose an object to be the subject of a poem (e.g., favorite animals, foods, shapes, flowers).
2. Lightly draw a simple outline of its shape on paper using a pencil.
3. Write the poem. Try not to make it too long—6 to 12 lines is a good length.
4. Pencil the poem into the shape, determining where you need more or fewer words to fit the shape.
5. Once you are satisfied with your poem, on a fresh piece of paper lightly draw the shape using a pencil.
6. Write the final draft in ink. Erase the outline of the shape, leaving only the words to create the image.

In a concrete poem there are no rules about rhyme or cadence. Most important are the shape created and words that reflect it. The web resources list at the end of this book contains a link to a good source for concrete poetry.

Epitaph

An epitaph is a poem that mourns someone's death. Usually it is intended for a person's tombstone, and more often than not it is a serious poem. In some cases, however, an epitaph tells a brief funny story in rhyme form. A funny epitaph poem often is only four lines long and makes fun of some aspect of a person's life, such as an unhealthy or bad habit. If it is well written, it sums up either an important message about the person's life or a core aspect of his or her personality. The following is an epitaph poem by Kenn Nesbitt.[3]

---

[3] "Chocolate Is Not a Vegetable," copyright © 2012 Kenn Nesbitt. All rights reserved. Reprinted by permission of the author.

Here lies poor Billy.
Although it sounds silly,
he never ate anything green.
The candy that filled him,
is also what killed him,
the day after last Halloween.

WRITING AN EPITAPH

Participants write a four-line epitaph.

1. Read some epitaph poems. (The web resources list at the end of this book contains a link to a good source for epitaphs.)
2. Choose a character or person to write about.
3. Note specifics about the person's life and personality, such as:
   - Quotes
   - Funny stories
   - History
   - Roles (e.g., father, mother, brother, sister, teacher)
   - How the person impacted lives
   - Qualities or accomplishments

Independent Activity

1. Create a four-line epitaph.
2. Put on an epitaph poetry reading.

Extended Activities

- Leave out the missing word or words that rhyme with the last word in the third line and challenge the group to come up with it.
- Research and make a list of epitaphs, leaving out the last word in the third line. Instruct the group to fill in the blanks.

Seasonal Activities

Exploring the seasons is fun and engaging. Each season has its own holidays, traditions, and weather conditions. Seasonal activities reinforce knowledge and understanding of the world. They also encourage us to go outdoors and explore the natural world. Following are a variety of fun seasonal activities.

❧ Hole-Punch Collage

Use a hole punch and colored paper to make a variety of collages. For winter pictures use white paper; for fall pictures use yellow, orange, red, and brown; for spring and summer choose pastel colors.

Materials

    Construction paper (seasonal colors)

    Glue sticks

HOLE-PUNCH COLLAGE
(TEMPERA PAINT VARIATION)

Hole punches

Pencils

Directions

1. Select a scene (e.g., winter: snowman, pine trees, snow scene, snow globe; spring: flowers, butterflies, rainbows, birds; summer: sun, ocean sailboat, fish; fall: pumpkin, leaves, ghost).
2. Use a pencil to draw the scene.
3. Use the hole punch on the construction paper to punch out numerous dots.
4. Use a glue stick to fill in the picture with hole-punched dots. Glue dots on the outline of the picture first.
5. *Optional:* Use other media such as crayons, colored pencils, watercolors, tempera paint, or colored chalk to enhance the background of the collage.

As a variation, use tempera paint and cotton swabs to create dot pictures.

⅊ Pressed and Dried Flowers

These can be used for pictures and stationery cards.

Materials

Construction paper and card stock

Pressed flowers and leaves

Glue

Directions

If possible, have participants collect flowers and leaves to press (steps 1 to 3).

1. At least a week ahead of time, pick flowers and/or collect leaves to press.
2. Press each bloom/leaf in a thick book. Telephone books work well. (Protect the pages with paper towels.)
3. When plants are pressed flat and dried, carefully remove them from the book.
4. Lay out an arrangement of flowers and/or leaves on card stock for stationery cards, or on construction paper for a picture to be framed.
5. Once you are satisfied with your arrangement, glue the plant material in place and allow to dry.

❧ Eggshell Planters

Make tiny eggshell planters for Easter or spring and grow tiny plants.

Materials

    Eggshells

    Paper egg cartons, straw, and potting soil

    Scissors

    Grass, bean, or flower seeds

    Egg dye, watercolors, tempera paint and paintbrushes, markers, or crayons

    Cups of water and paper towels (for dye and paint)

Directions

1. Choose media for designing eggshells (e.g., dye, crayons, watercolors).
2. Crack the eggs carefully leaving at least half of the shell intact.
3. Wash shells and place in egg carton to dry.
4. Dye and create a design on the eggshells.
5. Make a cardboard base for each eggshell. Glue shell to the base. Creatively decorate the base or cut out a variety of shapes (e.g., circle, flower, leaf shapes).
6. Fill shells half full with potting soil.
7. Plant and water seeds.

Eggshell Planters

❧ Eggshell Tulips

Create a bouquet of tulips. Use real eggshells or egg carton sections.

Materials

Eggshells or paper egg cartons

Scissors for egg carton

Glue

Markers

Tempera paint, paintbrushes, cups of water, paper towels

Green pipe cleaners

Ribbon

Directions

1. If using eggshells, clean them and allow time to dry. If using an egg carton, cut it into individual cups .
2. Decorate shells or carton with tempera paint and markers.
3. Twirl one end of pipe cleaner into a spiral shape and glue to eggshell, or poke a hole in the bottom of the carton and thread the pipe cleaner through, then twist.
4. Make a bouquet by tying flowers together with ribbon, or place flowers in an inexpensive vase.

❧ Guess What Region

Describe the weather in different regions. Note: Places in the Southern Hemisphere have winter weather during the months that there is summer weather in the Northern Hemisphere. In tropical areas near the equator, there are only two seasons: rainy and dry.

Directions

1. Research various regions.
2. Choose one region to describe.
3. See who can guess where it is.

Extended Activities

- Write about your favorite season and tell why it's a favorite.
- Illustrate a picture using a variety of media (e.g., collage using torn paper, watercolors, crayon resist, chalk).

❧ Pinecone Bird Feeder

Make a simple bird feeder from a pinecone.

Materials for each participant

1 large pinecone

24 inches of string

½ cup vegetable shortening

2½ cups cornmeal or oats

Birdseed

Directions

1. Tie string to pinecone.
2. Mix vegetable shortening and cornmeal or oats.
3. Cover pinecone with cornmeal or oat mixture.
4. Roll pinecone in birdseed.
5. Hang on tree branch for birds to eat.

❧ Pinecone Turkeys

Use a pinecone as the body of the turkey.

Materials for each participant

Turkey pattern

1 large pinecone

Small colored feathers

Construction paper (brown and yellow)

Googly eyes

Scissors

Glue

Directions

1. Using the pattern, draw turkey head and neck on brown construction paper and cut out.
2. Draw a beak on yellow construction paper and cut out.
3. Glue beak and googly eyes on turkey head.
4. With the pinecone on its side, glue the turkey head and neck onto the top (pointed end) of the pinecone.
5. Glue feathers onto the base (flat end) of the pinecone.
6. Use part of a red feather to make the wattle under the neck.

❧ SWEETHEARTS

This is a cooking activity for Valentine's Day that is good to do with young children and grandchildren.

Ingredients list for each participant

1 slice of bread

Strawberry jam

Heart-shaped cookie cutter

Raisins

Directions

1. Use cookie cutter to cut bread.
2. Spread strawberry jam on cut-out heart.
3. Make a face on the heart with raisins.

❧ THROWING SNOWBALLS

This activity is an icebreaker and reinforces language skills.

1. Write comments and riddles on white paper.
2. Ball up paper to look like a snowball.
3. Using a timer, begin a snowball fight.
4. When the timer goes off, have participants read the comment or answer the question on the nearest ball of paper.

❧ TEN BLACK DOTS

Create seasonal pictures using black dots. Use descriptive language to describe each picture.

Materials

1 package of adhesive black dots

Construction paper

White paper

Pencils and markers

Book: *Ten Black Dots* by Donald Crews (use to generate ideas)

TEN BLACK DOTS

Directed Instruction

1. Read *Ten Black Dots* to the group.
2. Brainstorm pictures to draw using 1 black dot, 2 black dots, 3 black dots, up to 10 dots.
3. Have participants draw a picture for each number of dots used, add the dots, and think of ways to describe each picture using colorful language.
4. Compile all pages into a book.
5. Brainstorm a creative title for the dot book.
6. Have participants share with other participants and grandchildren.

Examples

- One black dot can make the eye of a fish swimming on a hot summer day.
- Two black dots can make an owl perched on a tree branch on Halloween night.
- Three black dots can make the buttons of a snowman in a blanket of snow on a cold winter's day.
- Four black dots can make a garden of flowers sprouting on a beautiful spring morning.

❧ CHERRY BLOSSOM BRANCH

Paint a cherry blossom branch.

Materials

    Image of a cherry blossom branch

    White construction paper

    Pencils

    Tempera paint (red, white, and black)

    Paintbrushes (small, fine-tip, two different sizes)

    Cups of water and paper towels

    Writing paper

Directions

1. Display an image of a cherry blossom branch.
2. Make a rough sketch of a cherry blossom branch with a pencil.
3. Mix some of the white and red paint to make pink.
4. Paint four or five pink flowers—each having five petals—on the white construction paper.
5. Use the tip of the smaller brush to paint the branch. Begin painting the thickest part of the branch, then thin it out as the branch connects to each blossom.
6. Add smaller branches and buds.
7. Using red paint, highlight blossoms making sure that the center of each flower has the most red.
8. Use the tip of the smaller brush to paint pollen in the center of the blossoms.
9. Create a haiku poem to describe the cherry blossom branch.

❧ POPPIES

View paintings by Claude Monet and other impressionist artists, then create an impression of a field of poppies.

Materials

    Construction paper (green, black, white, red, and pink)

    Tempera paint (red and white)

    Paintbrushes, cups of water, paper towels

    Colored chalk

POPPIES

Directions
1. Choose construction paper for background.
2. Use colored chalk to make impressions of stems.
3. To create the flowers, dab white paint on the stems, then dab red paint over white to create a pinkish color.
4. Let dry.
5. Laminate and frame.

❧ FALL TREES
Create a tree illustrating the colors of fall, then write a poem.
Materials
   Construction paper (brown, white, and black)
   Tempera paint (green, red, orange, yellow, and brown)
   Paintbrushes, cups of water, paper towels
   1 thin sponge per participant
   Scissors
   Glue
   Writing paper, pencils, and pens
Directions
1. Choose white or black construction paper for background.
2. Cut sponge into 1-inch squares and dampen.

FALL TREES

3. Tear brown paper into small pieces.
4. Glue torn pieces of brown construction paper on background to create a mosaic tree trunk.
5. Sponge paint leaves on tree to create the colors of fall.
6. Think of ways to describe the fall tree in different forms of poetry and write poem.
7. Frame picture and glue poem on the back.

❧ SEASONAL HIGHLIGHTS

Create an outline of a seasonal picture on a watercolor background. Use descriptive language to describe the picture.

Materials

White construction paper

Watercolor paints, paintbrushes, cups of water, paper towels

Black permanent markers, fine and ultra-fine tips

Directed Instruction

Brainstorm ideas for simple pictures for each season. For example:

Winter: snowmen, pine trees, penguins, polar bears, snow-capped mountains

Spring: flowers, bunnies, butterflies, chicks, Easter baskets

Summer: fish, beach balls, palm trees, seashells

Fall: pumpkins, jack-o-lanterns, ghosts, bare trees, spiders, webs

Directions

1. Choose a season and sketch a drawing with a pencil.
2. Paint background with watercolors on white construction paper. Mix two or three colors.
3. Let paint dry and lightly draw picture with a pencil.
4. Outline picture with a permanent fine-tip black marker.
5. Describe the illustration in one sentence.
6. Write the sentence using a permanent black marker on the bottom edge of the paper.

ARRANGED COLLAGE

✺ARRANGED COLLAGE

Using rolled tissue paper, create a thematic collage.

Materials

Construction paper (various colors)

Green tissue paper

Pencils

Scissors

Glue

Directed Instruction

1. Brainstorm ideas and choose a theme (e.g., Easter: eggs; Halloween: jack-o-lanterns; Thanksgiving: turkeys; Christmas: trees).
2. Choose a color of construction paper for the background.
3. Draw and cut out various sizes and shapes of the theme picture.
4. Give each picture a different character by adding accessories (e.g., hair; glasses; hats; different-shaped eyes, noses, mouths).
5. Create a tissue vine to border the collage by tightly rolling the green tissue paper.
6. Cut out tissue leaves to add to the vine.
7. Frame picture using the tissue vine and leaves.

❧ SEASONAL TREES

Construct four trees using a variety of media to illustrate each season. Write descriptive words on the back to describe each season.

Materials

White and brown construction paper

Colored chalk

Cotton balls

Cotton swabs

Scissors

Glue

Tempera paint, paintbrushes, cups of water, paper towels

Pink tissue paper

Book: *My Favorite Time of Year* by Susan Pearson (use as a tool for visuals)

Directed Instruction

1. Read *My Favorite Time of Year* to the group.
2. Encourage participants to share seasonal changes related to their birthplace.
3. Brainstorm descriptive words for each season.
4. Fold white construction paper into equal sections accordion style.
5. Cut out or paint four tree trunks for each section.

SEASONAL TREES

6. Add different media to illustrate each season.

Spring: Glue on pink tissue for blossoms; paint or color green grass.

Summer: Use a cotton swab to paint leaves for the tree; use swab to add red cherries, add grass.

Fall: Use a cotton swab to paint fall-colored leaves on branches; also add leaves on ground.

Winter: Pull apart cotton balls to make snow and glue onto branches of the tree and on the ground.

7. Label each season or write descriptive words to illustrate each season.

8. Use colored chalk or oil pastels to highlight the background for each season.

❧ TREE TRUNK TREASURES: A SIMPLE FALL SCENE

Create a simple fall scene highlighting tree trunks.

Materials

Watercolor paints, paintbrushes, cups of water, paper towels

Crayons

Permanent black markers

White construction paper

Directions

1. Draw and color three very dark, tall tree trunks using a black crayon.

2. Add short branches of various sizes to both sides of each trunk.

TREE TRUNK TREASURES: A SIMPLE FALL SCENE (BY NORMA GONZALEZ)

3. Make a moon by using a permanent marker and tracing a large circle anywhere at the top of the paper.

4. Using a crayon, color the moon white or yellow.

5. Add images in the light of the moon (e.g., spider, spider web, ghostly shadow).

6. Add other night images to the picture using a permanent marker to create shadow effects.

7. Paint over picture using a mixture of blue or purple watercolor paint to make a background.

8. Using descriptive language, share and describe the picture in one sentence.

❧ TREE TRUNK TREASURES: A SIMPLE WINTER SCENE

Create a simple winter scene highlighting tree trunks.

Materials

Watercolor paints

White tempera paint

Paintbrushes, cups of water, paper towels

TREE TRUNK TREASURES: A SIMPLE WINTER SCENE

Masking tape

White construction paper

Directions

1. Create three or four tree trunks using masking tape.
2. Tear masking tape to add branches.
3. Paint around tape with blue watercolor paint to add a background.
4. Let paint dry.
5. Use cotton-tipped swab and white tempera paint and add dots of snow.
6. Peel off masking tape very carefully.
7. Using descriptive language, share and describe the picture in one sentence.

Abstract Art Activities

❧ SANDPAPER ART

Create a multicolored design using sandpaper.

Materials

    Pencils and paper for sketching

    Sandpaper sheets

    Crayons

    White construction paper

    Iron (standard household)

    Poster board

Directed Instruction

1. Discuss the origin of sand painting, which is the art of pouring colored sands and natural powdered pigments onto a surface to create a picture. This process often is referred to as *dry painting*. The technique is practiced by Native Americans in the Southwestern United States, Tibetan and Buddhist monks, and the Australian Aborigines.
2. Sketch a design.
3. Transfer the design onto sandpaper using crayons. Press down on the crayon firmly to ensure that the picture is dark and the design is colored in completely.
4. Place white construction paper over the design and use a hot iron to transfer the image to the construction paper.
5. Glue both designs side by side on poster board to create a mirror effect.
6. Frame the picture.

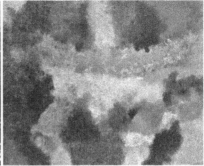

SANDPAPER ART. DESIGN ON SANDPAPER (LEFT); DESIGN
TRANSFERRED TO CONSTRUCTION PAPER (RIGHT)

NEWSPAPER ART
Design a city of tall buildings using newspaper print.
Materials
Newspaper
Construction paper (black and white)
Black felt-tip markers
Scissors
Glue
Directed Instruction
1. Present the materials and discuss ways to create a city using newspaper and black construction paper. Ask this question: What elements need to be incorporated to present the illusion of a city?
2. Sketch a design using rectangular shapes for buildings.
3. Cut out various sizes of rectangles from newspaper and black construction paper.
4. Arrange the shapes on white construction paper in an ABAB pattern (newspaper shape, corresponding black shape, newspaper shape, corresponding black shape) to create buildings and their shadows.
5. Glue buildings and shadows to the construction paper.
6. Use black felt-tipped marker to add windows to the newspaper buildings.
7. *Optional:* Use a black felt-tip marker to add other details (street, sun, clouds).

❧ Crayon Resist Design

Create an abstract design using a thick permanent marker on white construction paper.

Materials

    White construction paper (8 × 8 inches)

    Black construction paper

    Crayons

    Pencils

    Thick black permanent markers

    Watercolor paints, paintbrushes, cups of water, paper towels

    Glue

    Rulers

Directions

1. Think of ways to divide the white construction paper into a design using just lines (see example below for an idea).
2. Sketch the design onto the white construction paper using a pencil and a ruler.
3. Draw over the pencil design with a permanent marker.
4. Color each section of the design with crayons.
5. Paint over the crayon design with varied watercolor paints.
6. Cut out a frame for the picture using black construction paper.

CRAYON RESIST DESIGN

✣ SKETCHING HAIR

Practice sketching various styles of hair using a real-life subject.

Materials

White construction paper

Pencils

Erasers

Pens

Directions

1. Ask for a volunteer from the group to draw.
2. Outline the shape of the person's head using a pencil.
3. Add the neck and shoulders.
4. Examine the texture and lines of the hair.
5. Go over the outline of the head, neck, and shoulder with an ink pen.
6. Begin lightly drawing the strands of hair with a pencil.
7. Go over pencil marks with a pen.
8. Erase any exposed pencil marks.

SKETCHING HAIR

❧ Picture Collage

Create a collage using a variety of designs and illustrations.

Materials

    White construction paper

    Crayons, oil pastels, or colored pencils

    Rulers

    Scratch paper

Directed Instruction

1. Discuss favorite things and make a list.
2. Review different types of lines to create designs (e.g., spiral, zigzag, vertical, horizontal, slanted, curved).
3. Practice drawing pictures and designs for the collage.
4. Use a ruler to divide construction paper into several equal parts.
5. Decide on placement of pictures and designs.

Independent Practice

1. Sketch pictures and designs lightly with a pencil.
2. Color in pictures and designs with crayons, colored pencils, or oil pastels.

As a variation, paint over collage with watercolor paint.

PICTURE COLLAGE

❧ Positive/Negative Stencil

Discuss positive and negative things in life, then create a positive/negative stencil.

Materials

    Construction paper (various colors)

    Pencils

    Glue

    Scissors

Directed Instruction

1. Brainstorm positive and negative things in your life and make a list.
2. Discuss how each positive or negative thing has changed your life.
3. Choose a positive thing and a negative thing to write about. Questions to consider:

    How did it happen?

    Why did it happen?

    What would you change or do differently?

    What impact did it have on your life?

POSITIVE/NEGATIVE STENCIL

Independent Practice: Create a Positive/Negative Stencil

1. Choose two colors of construction paper: one for background and one for stencil.
2. Fold stencil construction paper in half.
3. Draw and cut out stencil.

4. Glue stencil on background construction paper.
5. On the back, write about one positive thing and one negative thing that have changed your life.

❧ CREATIVE SELF-IMAGES

Sketch a self-portrait from a headshot photograph. Write a description for each self-image.

Materials

Headshot photographs of participants
Large white construction paper
Thin black felt-tip markers
Colored chalk
Pencils
Scissors
Glue
White copy paper

Directed Instruction

1. Have participants practice sketching themselves using their headshot photograph.
2. After some practice, participants sketch their face on copy paper.
3. Print three or four copies of each participant's face.
4. Participants highlight each face with different colored chalk.
5. Participants cut out, arrange, and glue their faces on large white construction paper.
6. Using a black marker, participants add different types of lines to background to create a psychedelic effect.
7. Have participants share with the group and use descriptive words to describe the mood of each face.

CREATIVE SELF-IMAGES

✥ The Many Faces of Older Adults

Create faces using a variety of eyes, noses, mouths, eyebrows, and hair to symbolize different moods and personalities.

Materials

   Graph paper (1-inch square)

   White copy paper

   White construction paper

   Black construction paper for framing

   Colored pencils

   Thin black felt-tip markers

   Pipe cleaners, yarn, and string to create hair, eyelashes, and other features

   Scissors

   Glue

Directed Instruction

1. Brainstorm different moods and personalities and make a list.
2. Draw features (eyes, noses, and mouths) on copy paper to match different moods and personalities.
3. Choose features to create a face and cut them out.
4. On graph or construction paper, draw one or more faces and lay out eyes, nose, and mouth. (Graph paper can help with layout.)
5. Draw or add other details using pipe cleaners, yarn, and/or string to give the face more character.
6. Glue the features onto the face.
7. Frame face using a shadow box or paper frame.
8. Describe the mood and character of the different face or faces and share with the group.

As a variation, using the Create-A-Face worksheet on the following page, create unique portraits by assigning numbers to the different parts of a face. Participants roll a die and then draw the appropriate part. Each participant rolls the die 4 times.

Create-A-Face

roll...	a face	eyes	a nose	a mouth
⚀				
⚁				
⚂				
⚃				
⚄				
⚅				

Appendices

Appendix A. Additional Idioms, Commonly Misspelled Words, Food Words, and Recipes

IDIOMS

Beat a dead horse: To revive interest in a hopeless issue

Birds of a feather flock together: People of the same character or background tend to congregate.

Chicken out: To back out due to fear or the loss of nerve.

Chickens come home to roost: The consequences of wrongdoing always catch up with the wrongdoers.

Clay pigeon: A person easily cheated or taken advantage of.

Cook someone's goose: To ruin someone; to upset someone's plans.

Count one's chicken before they hatch: To make plans for events that might or might not happen.

Dark horse: An unexpectedly successful competitor.

Ducks in a row: To complete preparations; to become efficient and well organized.

Dumb bunny: A person who does something stupid; a term of endearment.

Early bird catches the worm: The one who arrives first has the best chance for success.

Eat crow: To be forced to admit a humiliating mistake.

Every dog has its day: Even the lowliest person sometimes achieves his or her goals.

From the horse's mouth: To obtain information from someone with first-hand knowledge of or expertise in the subject being discussed.

Get someone's goat: To annoy or anger someone (often deliberately).

Lame duck: An elected official whose term of office has not yet expired, but who has failed to be re-elected and therefore cannot gather much political support for initiatives.

Like water off a duck's back: Something faced easily and without apparent effort.

Neither fish nor fowl: Not one or the other; something that doesn't fit into any category being discussed.

Straw that broke the camel's back: The final annoyance or setback which—although minor—makes someone lose patience with the entire situation, task, person, or subject.

Wild goose chase: Frantically searching for something that is nearly impossible to find or obtain.

Commonly Misspelled Words

argument–arguement

because–becuase

believe–beleive

definitely–definiteley

ignorance–ignorence

intelligence–inteligence

library–librery

lightning–lightening

maintenance–maintenence

millennium–millenium

miracle–miracale

neighbor–neighbour

occasionally–occassionally

recommend–reccommend

schedule–scehedule

twelfth–twelth

weird–wierd

Food Words

Barbecue: Meat cooked with a spicy sauce on an outdoor grill. (From the Spanish name for the grill used to cook the meat. Originally came from the Taíno Indians of the Caribbean, who were conquered by the Spaniards.)

Coleslaw: A salad made of shredded cabbage and mayonnaise. (From the Dutch word *koosla*.)

Curry: A meat and vegetable dish made in a mixture of hot spices. (From the Indian word *kari*. Explorers brought curry from India.)

Frankfurter: A hot dog. (After the city of Frankfurt, Germany.)

Hamburger: A ground beef patty. (After the city of Hamburg, Germany.)

Kebab: Meat and vegetables marinated and cooked on a skewer. (From the Turkish word *kebap*.)

Pickle: A cucumber that has been preserved in vinegar or salt. (From the Dutch word *pekel*.)

Salsa: A spicy tomato sauce flavored with onions and peppers. (A Spanish word that comes from the Latin word for salt. Latin was the language of ancient Romans. Salt was used by the Romans to flavor food.)

Spaghetti: Form of pasta made from flour and water. (From Italy; it adds the meaning "little" to the word *spago*, which means "cord.")

Strudel: A German word for a pastry that has a fruit or cheese filling. (The original German word means "whirlpool," intimating a whirlpool of tasty delights on the tongue.)

Tofu: A soft food made from soybeans that is high in protein. (From China and Japan.)

Other words to research: guacamole, tamale, tomato, sushi, papaya, ketchup, pasta.

RECIPES

❧ PEANUT BUTTER BALLS

Ingredients

¼ cup peanut butter

¼ cup oatmeal

¼ cup dried cranberries

¼ cup sunflower seeds

2 teaspoons honey

Optional: ¼ cup powdered milk

Directions

1. Mix peanut butter, oatmeal, dried cranberries, sunflower seeds, and (optional) powdered milk.
2. Stir in honey, 1 teaspoon at a time, until texture is proper for rolling.
3. Roll mixture into balls and place on cookie sheet.
4. Refrigerate for at least 30 minutes.

❧ FLAKY PEANUT BUTTER COOKIES

Ingredients

½ cup corn syrup

½ cup sugar

¾ cup peanut butter

2½ cups cornflakes

Directions

Work with a partner.

1. Mix corn syrup and sugar in a microwave-safe bowl.
2. Melt mixture in the microwave and bring it to a slight boil for about 1 minute.
3. Remove bowl from microwave and add peanut butter and cornflakes to mixture.
4. Stir briskly.
5. Drop mixture by tablespoon on wax paper.
6. Let cool and share with partner.

❧ PEANUT BUTTER CRISPIES

Ingredients

½ cup corn syrup

½ cup sugar

1 cup peanut butter

1 cup chow mein noodles, crumbled

Directions

Work with a partner.

1. Mix corn syrup and sugar in microwave-safe bowl.
2. Melt mixture in microwave and bring to a slight boil for about 1 minute.
3. Remove bowl from microwave and add crumbled chow mein noodles and peanut butter to mixture.
4. Drop mixture by tablespoon on wax paper. Makes about a dozen.
5. Let cool and share with partner.

❧ CHOCOLATE CHOW MEIN

Ingredients

¼ cup peanut butter

¼ cup chocolate chips

¼ cup butter

3 cups chow mein noodles

3 cups Corn, Rice, or Wheat Chex cereal

1 cup chopped nuts

2 cups confectioners' sugar

Directions

1. Melt peanut butter, chocolate chips, and butter in a microwavable bowl.
2. Put chow mein noodles, Chex cereal, and nuts in a resealable plastic bag.
3. Pour melted peanut butter, chocolate, and butter into chow mein mixture.
4. Shake to coat.
5. Add sugar and shake again.
6. Remove from plastic bag and form into balls.
7. Eat and enjoy!

❧ TURKEY MATZO

Ingredients

6 matzo crackers

6 small slices of turkey

¼ cup shredded cheddar cheese

1 tablespoon olive oil

Salt, pepper, and dried rosemary

Directions

1. Brush matzo crackers with olive oil.
2. Sprinkle with salt, pepper, and rosemary.
3. Top with sliced turkey.
4. Sprinkle on shredded cheddar cheese.
5. Bake 5 minutes at 400°F.

Chocolate Nut Clusters
Ingredients
- ¼ cup unsalted roasted nuts
- 1 ounce chocolate chips

Directions
1. Melt chocolate chips in microwave.
2. Mix nuts and chocolate together.
3. Spoon and drop on wax paper.
4. Refrigerate until set.

Veggie Wraps
Ingredients
- 1 flour tortilla
- 1 tomato
- ½ cup spinach leaves
- ½ avocado, chopped
- ¼ cup pico de gallo (see recipe below)
- 1 teaspoon Italian dressing
- Sliced cheddar cheese

Directions
1. Layer ingredients on tortilla in this order: tomato, spinach, avocado, pico de gallo, cheese, and Italian dressing.
2. Wrap ingredients in tortilla.
3. Slice wrapped tortilla into quarters.

Pico de Gallo
Ingredients
- 4 ripe tomatoes
- 1 small onion
- ½ cup cilantro leaf
- 2 or 3 jalapeño peppers
- 1 tablespoon lime juice
- Salt and pepper

Directions
1. Finely chop tomatoes, onion, cilantro, and jalapeño peppers.
2. Mix all ingredients together.
3. Cover and refrigerate until chilled.

❧ CHEESE BALLS
Ingredients
1 cup shredded Swiss cheese
1 cup shredded cheddar cheese
4 ounces cream cheese, softened
¼ cup sour cream
¼ cup chopped onion
1 ounce pimiento, undrained
5 slices crispy cooked bacon, crumbled into bits
¼ cup finely chopped pecans
⅛ teaspoon salt
⅛ teaspoon pepper
2 tablespoons parsley flakes
1 teaspoon poppy seeds

Directions
1. Bring Swiss and cheddar cheese to room temperature.
2. Mix cream cheese and sour cream and beat until fluffy.
3. Add Swiss cheese, cheddar cheese, onion, pimiento (undrained), ½ cup bacon bits, ½ cup pecans, salt, and pepper. Beat until blended completely.
4. Cover and chill until firm.
5. Shape mixture into one large ball on wax paper.
6. In a small bowl combine the remaining bacon, parsley, and poppy seeds.
7. Spread bacon, parsley, and poppy seed mixture on wax paper.
8. Roll cheese ball in mixture to coat.
9. Wrap ball and chill.
10. Let stand 30 minutes at room temperature before serving.
11. Serve with crackers.

Appendix B. Questionnaires

NEW RESIDENT QUESTIONNAIRE

1. What is your name? _____
2. How old are you? When is your birthday? _____
3. What is your relationship status? _____
4. Do you have any siblings? If yes, how many? _____
5. How many children do you have? What are their names? _____
6. How many grandchildren do you have? Great-grandchildren? _____
7. What is your heritage? _____
8. What was your last occupation? _____
9. Are you allergic to anything? If yes, what? _____
10. Do you wear glasses or contacts? _____
11. Have you ever broken a bone? _____
12. Are you right- or left-handed? _____
13. Do you have a nickname? If yes, what is it? _____
14. Do you smoke? _____
15. What time do you get up in the morning? _____
16. Do you shower daily? _____
17. Do you have any pets? _____
18. What is your favorite food? _____
19. What is your least favorite food? _____
20. What annoys you? _____
21. What are your fears? _____
22. Do you have any hidden talents? _____
23. What do you like to do in your spare time? _____
24. What goal would you like to achieve this year? _____
25. Describe yourself in three words. _____

ACTIVITY QUESTIONNAIRE

1. What is your name? _____
2. What is your favorite sport? _____
3. What is your favorite website? _____
4. What is your skill level for using technology? 1 = poor; 10 = excellent _
5. What is your favorite book? Magazine? _____
6. What style of music do you like? _____
7. What is your favorite song(s)? _____
8. What song mostly describes your life now? _____
9. Who is your favorite artist/performer? _____
10. What is your favorite TV show? Movie? _____
11. What is your favorite pet/animal? _____
12. What is your favorite food? _____
13. What is your favorite dessert? _____
14. What is your favorite ice cream flavor? _____
15. Do you exercise? How do you feel about exercising? ____
16. What do you do for fun? _____
17. What is your favorite thing to do on a hot summer day? ____
    On a cold winter day? _____
18. What makes you happy/sad/mad/scared? _____
19. What is your favorite season/holiday? _____
20. What was your favorite subject in school? _____
21. What hidden talents do you have? _____
22. On a scale of 1–10, how bored are you? _____
23. What activities would you be interested in? _____

Informational Questionnaire

1. Name: _____

2. Skills and/or talents: _____

3. Political viewpoint: _____

4. Best subjects in school: _____

5. Favorite books: _____

6. Favorite magazines: _____

7. Favorite TV shows: _____

8. Favorite movies: _____

9. Favorite actors: _____

10. Favorite singers: _____

11. Travel experience: _____

12. Favorite era: _____

13. Favorite city/state/country: _____

14. Favorite hero: _____

15. Favorite season/holiday: _____

Interview Questions

1. What is your name? _____

2. Where were you born? In what year? _____

3. Are you married? _____

4. Do you have children/grandchildren/great-grandchildren? _____

5. Do you have siblings? _____

6. Do you look more like your mom or your dad? _____

7. What is your heritage? _____

8. Do you have any pets? If so, how many and what are their names? _____

9. What schools did you attend? _____

10. What is your level of education? _____

11. What was your last occupation? _____

12. What is your favorite quote? _____

13. What are your life goals? _____

14. What is the best advice you've ever received? _____

15. What is the best thing you've ever been given in life? _____

16. If you could go back in time and change or see something, when and what would it be? _____

17. Do you have any regrets in life? _____

18. Do you have any talents? _____

19. Who is your hero? _____

20. Describe yourself in three words. _____

Appendix C. Graphic Organizers

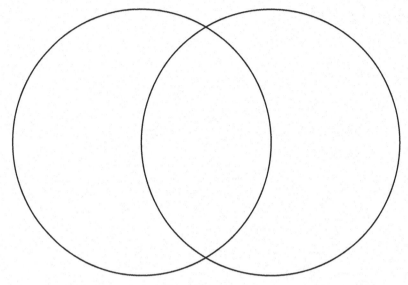

VENN DIAGRAM

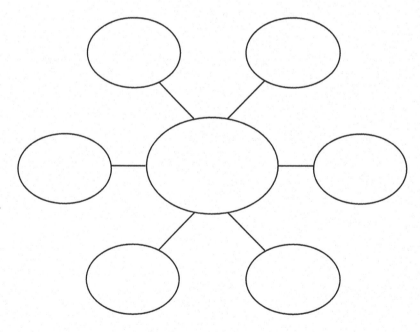

WORD WEB

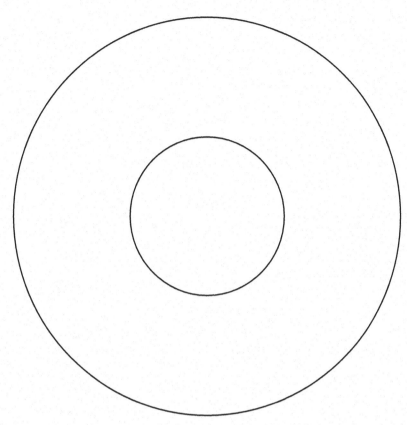

CIRCLE MAP

More healthy food choices

Changes we could make

Music on Fridays

CIRCLE MAP EXAMPLE

TREE MAP

Changes we could make

Activities   *Meals*   *Rules*

TREE MAP EXAMPLE

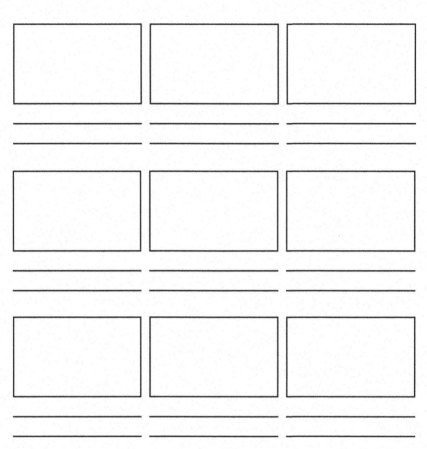

STORYBOARD

Appendix D. Sample Daily and Weekly Plans

SAMPLE DAILY SCHEDULE
LANGUAGE ARTS

Monday	10:00 a.m. Oral language warm-up activities	2:00 p.m. Oral language: listening lessons
Tuesday	10:00 a.m. Written language warm-up activities	2:00 p.m. Written language: expository, descriptive, narrative, or persuasive writing
Wednesday	10:00 a.m. Oral language warm-up activities	2:00 p.m. Oral language: speaking lessons
Thursday	10:00 a.m. Language-related art projects or cooking activities	2:00 p.m. Written language: poetry
Friday	10:00 a.m. Vocabulary building	2:00 p.m. Total physical response (TPR) activities: music, movement, rhythms

SAMPLE WEEKLY SCHEDULE
LANGUAGE ARTS

The following pages contain three sample weekly schedules with activities and lessons.

WEEK 1 MONDAY

10:00 a.m. Oral Language Warm-Up Activities	2:00 p.m. Listening Lessons
ACTIVATING PRIOR KNOWLEDGE (P. 9) Read a poem or selection from a story or show a picture to trigger memories from the participants' past. Ask the group to respond with their own memories. **PARAPHRASING (P. 11)** • Read a poem or selection from a story, then ask for a volunteer to paraphrase the selection. • Show a picture and ask a participant to describe it. Then, ask for a volunteer to paraphrase the description.	**SOLVING MYSTERIES (P. 24)** Given a mystery scenario with clues, participants work together to solve the mystery. 1. Each participant chooses his or her favorite mystery to present to the group. 2. The participant presents the scenario to the group and points out the clues. 3. The group works together or breaks up into smaller groups to solve the mystery. **PREDICTING ENDINGS (P. 24)** Participants predict or change endings to stories. 1. Introduce a new novel or short story to the group. 2. Read one chapter at a time without giving away the chapter ending. Ask critical-thinking questions as you read. 3. Brainstorm ideas for the chapter or story ending. 4. Read the ending, then compare and contrast with group predictions. 5. Repeat the process for remaining chapters.

WEEK 1 TUESDAY

10:00 a.m. Written Language Warm-Up Activities	2:00 p.m. Writing Lessons
❧ SPELLING GAMES (P. 47) For example, Don't Misspell "Misspell." Make double-sided cards, one side with the correct spelling and the other with the incorrect spelling. (See pp. 47-48 for the full activity.)	❧ WRITING AN EXPOSITORY ESSAY (P. 50) Choose a topic, such as how technology has changed the lives of seniors. Write an introductory paragraph containing the main idea (the thesis). In the next three paragraphs, provide details to support the thesis. In the last paragraph, restate the thesis and tie together the major points of the essay. (See pp. 50–51 for the full lesson.)

WEEK 1 WEDNESDAY

10:00 a.m. Oral Language Warm-Up Activities	2:00 p.m. Speaking Lessons
❧ SEQUENCING (P. 12) Read a story to the group, then have the group members retell the story. This can be done in a round-robin session with everyone seated in a circle. Another option is to draw numbers to determine the order. Choose one person to be the recorder. As each person tells the story, the recorder writes down the responses. After everyone has had a turn, the recorder reads the responses to the group. Next, reread the story, comparing it to the recorder's notes to confirm that the details are in sequence.	❧ THE MAGIC WAND (P. 31) 1. Tell the group: You have just found a magic wand that allows you to make three community-related changes. You can change anything you want—for example, physical appearance, activities, staffing, food, rules. 2. Brainstorm possible changes to make. 3. Chart changes using a graphic organizer, such as a word web, tree map, circle map, or list. (See appendix C for templates.) (See pp. 31–32 for the full lesson.)

WEEK 1 THURSDAY

10:00 a.m. Language-Related Art or Cooking Activities	2:00 p.m. Writing Lessons
❧ TASTY MAGIC WANDS (P. 17) *Ingredients list for each participant* 2 pretzel rods ⅓ cup chopped nuts, dried fruit, and/ or crushed frosty flakes cereal Peanut butter to taste *Directions* 1. Spread peanut butter on a few inches of the pretzel rod. 2. Roll the rods in chopped nuts, dried fruit, or frosty flakes. (Mixing and matching is fun and tasty, too!)	❧ ACROSTIC POETRY (P. 62) 1. Decide on a subject word or phrase for the poem. 2. Write the subject vertically on the page. 3. Think about words or phrases that describe the subject that start with a letter in the subject name. 4. Continue filling in the rest of the lines to create a poem. 5. The lines should relate to one other. 6. The poem should make sense. For example, "dad": Dependable And Delightful (See pp. 62–63 for the full lesson.)

Week 1 Friday

10:00 a.m. Oral Language Warm-Up Activities	2:00 p.m. TPR Activities
❧ INCOMPLETE SENTENCES (P. 39) Take turns completing sentences orally. Construct sentences that indicate a word's meaning, such as: It's fun to be at a jovial event because _____. A dinosaur is a titanic animal because _____. What would make a person shout, "Eureka!"? _____ New activities directors might need a mentor because _____. A makeup artist might need a muse because _____. Fatalities might occur when _____. The politician felt the fury of the people when _____. As a variation, list words on a chart and provide a point value for each word. Give participants an incomplete sentence and ask them to find the word on the chart that completes the sentence.	❧ TOTAL PHYSICAL RESPONSE (TPR) (P. 16) Given commands using directional words, participants follow oral directions. *Guided Practice* • Call out exercises using directional words. For example: "Bend your right arm up and down; twist your left foot counterclockwise." • Add music to give the exercises more flair. *Independent Activities* • Have participants take turns giving directions. • A variation is to present open-ended directions: "What part of your body can go up and down? What can bend . . . twist . . . slide . . . stretch . . . shake . . . move back and forth or side to side?" (See p. 16 for the full lesson.)

Week 2 Monday

10:00 a.m. Oral Language Warm-Up Activities	2:00 p.m. Listening Lessons
❧ Recounting Experiences (p. 11) Ask the participants to share events or milestones in their lives. Possible topics: Your earliest memory. When you were a child. . . . Something that made you happy or sad. If you could change one thing in your life. . . .	❧ Follow My Lead (p. 15) Given oral directions, participants draw a picture. 1. Display a few simple drawings or pictures. 2. Have the group decide picture which they would like to draw. 3. Display the picture and model step by step how to draw it. 4. Keeping the picture displayed, have the group draw the picture following your verbal cues. (See pp. 15–16 for the full lesson.)

Week 2 Tuesday

10:00 a.m. Written Language Warm-Up Activities	2:00 p.m. Writing Lessons

❧ Describe the Seasons (p. 45)
List nouns, verbs, and adjectives to describe seasons. For example:
Winter
  Nouns: snow, hot chocolate, jackets, scarves, sleds
  Adjectives: cold, windy, icy, snowy, freezing
  Verbs: skate, ski, freeze
Spring
  Nouns: flowers, butterflies, bunnies, raindrops
  Adjectives: green, fresh, colorful, cheerful
  Verbs: rain, grow, clean, drizzle
Summer
  Nouns: beach, pool, sun
  Adjectives: hot, bright, sunny, humid
  Verbs: sweat, swim, surf
Fall
  Nouns: leaves, rake, pumpkin, acorns
  Adjectives: cloudy, orange, colorful
  Verbs: harvest, pick, trick or treat
Extended Activities
Write about a favorite season, then illustrate the season using a variety of media (e.g., collage, watercolors, crayon resist, oil pastels).
	❧ Writing a Descriptive Essay (p. 52)
	A descriptive essay describes something (e.g., an object, a person, a place, an experience, an emotion, or a situation). It paints a vivid picture in the reader's mind and appeals to the senses through the process of describing how something looks, sounds, feels, smells, and tastes.
	
	Select a subject: Make detailed observation notes on your subject. If it is a place, try to visit and record how it looks, sounds, and smells. Appeal to the senses. Take time to brainstorm; for example, if you are describing your favorite food, choose words that are connected to the food (for instance, pizza: sauce, cheese, crust, pepperoni spices, steaming, melted). After making a list, begin compiling descriptive lists for each word. Consider this: If the reader begins craving the pizza, the goal of the essay has been achieved. (See p. 52 for the full lesson.)

Week 2 Wednesday

10:00 a.m. Oral Language Warm-Up Activities	2:00 p.m. Speaking Lessons
❧ Describing and Explaining (p. 9) Start a discussion about something the participants can either describe or explain. For example: Describe the perfect meal. Explain how to cook your favorite dish. Describe the perfect senior community. Explain the steps of a favorite craft. Describe a pet peeve. Explain why you find it irritating or annoying. Describe a favorite place. Explain why it's a favorite. Describe the perfect mate.	**❧ Imaginary Ball (p. 33)** Participants think, listen, and pay attention to details. *Instructions* 1. Have the group sit in a circle. 2. Choose one person to hold an imaginary ball. 3. That person says the name of another person in the group, then "tosses the ball" to that person while saying the first word that comes to mind. For example, "heart." The person who catches the ball then says a word associated with that word (e.g., "valentine," "love," "beat"). 4. The group continues tossing the ball and making word associations until everyone has had a turn.

WEEK 2 THURSDAY

10:00 a.m. Language-Related Art or Cooking Activities	2:00 p.m. Writing Lessons
❧ APPLE CRESCENT TREATS (P. 18) *Ingredients list for each participant* 1 apple ⅓ cup granola Peanut butter to taste Honey to taste *Directions* 1. Slice apples into crescents. 2. Spread with peanut butter. 3. Press granola on top. 4. Drip honey over granola.	❧ WRITING A CINQUAIN (P. 65) Participants write a cinquain following a simple model. *Directed Instruction* 1. Introduce the group to a variety of cinquains. (The web resources list toward the back of this book contains a link to a good source for cinquains.) 2. Choose a subject to write about as a group, such as: Favorite things Things you dislike Something you see around you Something that happens to you 3. Brainstorm words or phrases associated with the subject. 4. Think about the story you want to convey to the reader. 5. Write the words and phrases in an order that tells the story. Here's an example of a cinquain about Jell-O that follows format 3. Jell-O Cold and yummy It wiggles and it shakes As it flows through the hungry child's Tummy (See pp. 65–66 for the full lesson.)

Week 2 Friday

10:00 a.m. Oral Language Warm-Up Activities	2:00 p.m. TPR Activities
❧ Matching Prefixes and Suffixes (p. 39) 1. Color-code index cards with prefixes, suffixes, and meanings. 2. Match prefixes with correct meaning. 3. Match suffixes with correct meaning. **❧ Recalling Words (p. 39)** 1. Write prefixes and suffixes on index cards. 2. Separate cards into suffix and prefix piles. 3. Have participants or groups draw from one pile and think of a word containing that prefix or suffix. Give extra points if a player is able to use the word in a sentence.	**❧ Total Physical Response (TPR) (p. 16)** Given commands using directional words, participants follow oral directions. *Guided Practice* • Call out exercises using directional words. For example: "Bend your right arm up and down; twist your left foot counterclockwise." • Add music to give the exercises more flair. *Independent Activities* • Have participants take turns giving directions. • A variation is to present open-ended directions: "What part of your body can go up and down? What can bend . . . twist . . . slide . . . stretch . . . shake . . . move back and forth or side to side?" (See p. 16 for the full lesson.)

WEEK 3 MONDAY

10:00 a.m. Oral Language Warm-Up Activities	2:00 p.m. Listening Lessons
❧ SELF-ESTEEM (P. 11) Lead a discussion that helps build self-esteem. Help participants feel comfortable talking about themselves by asking questions such as: How would you describe yourself? What is your best quality? What are you an expert at doing? What would you like to learn? Why? What traits do you admire in others? Why? When do you feel special? How can others help you? What makes a good friend?	❧ BEADING NECKLACES (P. 14) Given an oral description of each bead, participants create a necklace with a specific pattern. *Guided Practice* Have the group practice listening to the description of various beads and locating them in a pile. A variation is to have the group practice describing beads by placing a number of beads in a baggie and having each participant pull out one and describe it to the group. *Independent Activity* 1. Provide each person with a small baggie of decorative beads and a 16-inch-long string for beading. 2. Inform the group that each participant is creating a necklace. (If time is short, have the group create bracelets.) 3. The objective is to string the beads in the order given, based on description. 4. Remind the participants to listen very carefully to be able choose the correct bead. 5. After the activity is complete, each person has the option of keeping the design (you can add a clasp) or creating his or her own pattern.

WEEK 3 TUESDAY

10:00 a.m. Written Language Warm-Up Activities	2:00 p.m. Writing Lessons
❧ SIMILES (P. 46) Have you ever heard these expressions: "Sharp as a tack" or "Fit as a fiddle"? These are similes Fill in the blanks in the phrases below. Try to create original expressions. As funny as _____. As loud as _____. As nervous as _____. As wet as _____. As hard as _____. As quiet as _____. As smart as _____. As cool as _____. As crooked as _____. As bright as _____.	❧ WRITING AN ADVERTISEMENT (P. 54) Participants use a print or television advertisement as a guide for designing their own advertisement for a product to enhance their community. *Guided Practice: Write a Critique* 1. Identify the strengths and weaknesses of the advertisement. What are the strongest and weakest components of its persuasive argument? 2. Make a list of persuasive words. 3. Identify the targeted audience. 4. Define the main message the writer wants the audience to know about the product. 5. Determine the tone (e.g., funny, silly, serious, or informative). *Independent Activity: Create Your Own Advertisement* Create an advertisement to enhance your community. Make sure all of the elements of a persuasive essay are included. (See pp. 54–55 for the full lesson.)

WEEK 3 WEDNESDAY

10:00 a.m. Oral Language Warm-Up Activities	2:00 p.m. Speaking Lessons
❧ FIRSTS (P. 10) Every person has had and has done many things for first time: first pet, first love, first school, first home, first job. Ask questions to generate discussions that bring back memories and activate prior knowledge. A variation is to have participants think of phrases that incorporate firsts: First comes the puppy, then the [dog]. First comes the seed, then the [tree]. First comes the tadpole, then the [frog]. First comes the smile, then the [friend].	❧ MEMORIES (P. 33) Participants talk about favorite memories. This activity requires dice: one die for each participant. *Instructions* 1. Choose an era for each number on the die (e.g., '50s = 1, '60s = 2, '70s = 3). 2. Have the group take turns rolling their die and thinking of a memory from the corresponding era. 3. Ask the following questions about the memory: What time of year was it? What scents were in the air? Where were you? Who was with you? How did you feel? What made this day different? Vary the activity by choosing another topic, such as happiest time, proudest moment, best vacation, first love, most embarrassing moment.

Week 3 Thursday

10:00 a.m. Language-Related Art or Cooking Activities	2:00 p.m. Writing Lessons
❧ Fruit Salad Tree (p. 21) *Ingredients list for each participant* 1 lettuce leaf 1 slice pineapple ½ banana 1 small can fruit cocktail, or sliced fresh fruit Grapes *Directions* 1. Place lettuce leaf on plate. 2. Place slice of pineapple in center of lettuce. 3. Place banana vertically in center of pineapple. 4. Drain fruit cocktail. 5. Put fruit cocktail and grapes on toothpicks. 6. Arrange skewered fruit on banana. 7. Discuss other salads that could be made with fruit. 8. Discuss "First comes the tree, then comes the...."	❧ Writing a Haiku (p. 69) Participants write a haiku inspired by nature. *Directed Instruction* 1. As a group, read a variety of haiku poems about nature. 2. Review the characteristics of haiku. 3. Take a nature walk and tune into the surroundings. Have participants carry a notebook and write down lines that come to them. 4. Ask these questions: Which details in the environment spark an interest? What makes them stand out? 5. For the first haiku, participants should adhere to the 5-7-5 pattern. After mastering the writing of a haiku, they may branch out and use other patterns. 6. Share haikus with the group. (See pp. 69–70 for the full lesson.)

WEEK 3 FRIDAY

10:00 a.m.	2:00 p.m.
Oral Language Warm-Up Activities	TPR Activities

❧ IDENTIFYING SYNONYMS (P. 41)

The following list can help to get the activity started. Extend the lesson by giving extra points if the person can provide a synonym for the word that does not belong in the group (the <u>underlined</u> words in the following list).

successful: thriving triumphant flourishing <u>destitute</u>

weird: odd bizarre unusual <u>ordinary</u>

evil: diabolical <u>virtuous</u> malevolent heinous

special: exceptional novel <u>mediocre</u> unique

important: crucial momentous <u>inconsequential</u> imperative

clean: <u>contaminated</u> immaculate pristine tidy

warm: affectionate compassionate <u>apathetic</u> tender

active: energetic animated vigorous <u>dormant</u>

cranky: irritable <u>amiable</u> cantankerous fractious

busy: engaged industrious occupied <u>indolent</u>

❧ TOTAL PHYSICAL RESPONSE (TPR) (P. 16)

Given commands using directional words, participants follow oral directions.

Guided Practice

- Call out exercises using directional words. For example: "Bend your right arm up and down; twist your left foot counterclockwise."

- Add music to give the exercises more flair.

Independent Activities

- Have participants take turns giving directions.

- A variation is to present open-ended directions: "What part of your body can go up and down? What can bend . . . twist . . . slide . . . stretch . . . shake . . . move back and forth or side to side?"

(See p. 16 for the full lesson.)

Glossary

Adjective: A describing word. Adjectives modify nouns and denote what kind, what color, which one, or how many (e.g., the *red* balloon; the *tallest* building; a *breathtaking* view).

Antonym: A word of opposite meaning (e.g., *big* is an antonym for *little*).

Climax: The most intense, exciting, or important part of a story that usually takes place at or near the end.

Descriptive Writing: Writing that uses vivid language to evoke sights, sounds, smells, tastes, and textures.

Expository Writing: Writing that explains, describes, gives information, or informs in an organized manner. It is considered the most common form of writing. Effective expository writing contains a main idea, supporting details, and a conclusion.

Figurative Language: Language that uses figures of speech—words or expressions with a meaning that differs from the literal interpretation—to make an impact. Idioms, metaphors, similes, and personification are all types of figurative language.

    Idiom: An expression that cannot be understood from the meanings of its individual words. For example, "It's raining cats and dogs" means that it is raining very hard.

    Metaphor: A figure of speech in which a word or phrase is applied to an object or action to which it is not literally applicable. It is an implied or hidden comparison between two things or objects that are not alike but have common characteristics (e.g., "You are my shining star"). The person described doesn't actually produce physical light but rather is someone who brings happiness or joy.

    Personification: Giving human qualities to nonhuman things (e.g., "The flower opened its petals and winked at me").

Simile: Comparing two things using *like* or *as*. Similes help to create a mental picture (e.g., "The wind howls like a wolf on the prowl"; "She was as white as a ghost").

Multiple Meanings: Words that have more than one meaning. This includes homographs, homonyms, and homophones.

Homograph: One of two or more words that are spelled identically, but that have different meanings and word forms, and possibly have different pronunciation (e.g., *lead:* the metal; *lead:* the verb for going ahead).

Homonym: One of two or more words having the same spelling and pronunciation, but have different meanings and origins (e.g., *stalk:* to harass a person; *stalk:* a part of a plant; *rose:* a flower, *rose:* past tense of rise).

Homophone: One of two or more words that have the same pronunciation but have different meanings, origins, or spellings (e.g., *to, too, two*).

Noun: A word that is the name of something (e.g., a person, place, animal, thing, quality, action, or concept). Usually used in a sentence as the subject or object of a verb.

Narrative/Narrative Writing: A story or account of events and experiences, whether true or fictitious. Narrative essays are often anecdotal and personal.

Persuasive Writing: Writing that presents an opinion, reasons, and examples to influence action or thought.

Plot: The sequence of events in a story. Includes the opening event (what happens at the beginning of the story, or the primary problem that the main character faces), the rising action, the climax, the falling action, and the resolution.

Poetry: Writing that speaks to the senses and creates an emotional response through meaning, sound, and rhythm.

Prefix: An affix attached to the beginning of a word, base, or phrase used to produce a derivative word. The prefix in the word *recall* is *re*. (The root word is *call*.) See **Root Word** and **Suffix**.

Root Word: A root, or root word, is a word that does not have a prefix (attached to the beginning of a word) or a suffix (attached to the end of a word). The root sometimes is referred to as the base of the word. For example, *call* is the base of the word *recalling. Re* is the prefix and *ing* is the suffix.

Setting: The environment in which a story takes place, including the period, the location, and the physical characteristics of the surroundings.

Suffix: An affix attached to the end of a word, base, or phrase used to produce a derivative word. The suffix in the word *calling* is *ing.* (The root word is *call.*) See **Root Word** and **Prefix.**

Syllable: A single unit of the written or spoken word that creates an unbroken sound. For example, the word *little* contains two syllables: *lit* + *tle.* Syllables give rhythm and depth to poetic sentences.

Synonym: A word or phrase that means the same or nearly the same as another word or phrase (e.g., *tiny* is a synonym for *little*).

Theme: The main message or moral of a story.

Tone: The attitude the author adopts with regard to a specific character, place, or development, such as excited, sad, nervous, curious, disappointed, or serious. For example, who would most likely have a serious tone—a police officer, a comedian, or a friend?

Verb: A word that expresses an action, an occurrence, or a state of being (e.g., *run, jump, think, happen, exist*).

Vivid Language: Describing things using colorful language that paints a picture in a reader's mind. Vivid language helps the reader clearly envision what the author is talking about.

Resources

Web

POETRY

Acrostic (http://examples.yourdictionary.com/acrostic-poem-examples.html)

Ballad (http://www.webexhibits.org/poetry/explore_famous_ballad_examples
.html; http://www.studyguide.org/ballad_examples.htm)

Cinquain (www.readwritethink.org/files/resources/lesson_images/lesson43/RW
T016-1.PDF)

Concrete (Shape) (http://www.shadowpoetry.com/resources/wip/shape.html)

Couplet (www.poetrysoup.com/poems/Couplet)

Diamante (http://pages.uoregon.edu/leslieob/diamantes.html; www.eduplace.com
/activity/pdf/diamante_poetry.pdf)

Epitaph (literaryterms.net/epitaph)

Haiku (http://examples.yourdictionary.com/examples-of-haiku-poems.html)

Limerick (http://www.webexhibits.org/poetry/explore_famous_limerick_exam
ples.html)

FOLKLORE, TONGUE TWISTERS, AND IDIOMS

Folktales and Folklore (http://www.americanfolklore.net/sindex.html)

Myths (http://myths.e2bn.org/mythsandlegends/showcase.html)

Tongue Twisters (https://www.engvid.com/english-resource/50-tongue-twisters
-improve-pronunciation/; www.uebersetzung.at/twister/en.htm; americanfolk
lore.net/folklore/2010/07/funny_tongue_twisters.html)

Idioms (www.smart-words.org/quotes-sayings/idioms-meaning.htm; www.eslcafe
.com/idioms/id-list.html; www.idiomsite.com)

Publications of Interest

Cognitive Aging: Progress in Understanding and Opportunities for Action (thescience
experience.org/Books/Cognitive_Aging.pdf)

"Education May Cut Dementia Risk, Study Finds" (https://www.nytimes.com
/2016/02/11/health/education-may-cut-dementia-risk-study-finds.html)

"A Lifetime of Intellectual Stimulation Staves Off Dementia" (http://www.psmag
.com/navigation/health-and-behavior/lifetime-intellectual-stimulation
-staves-dementia-84088/)

"New Insights into the Dementia Epidemic" (https://doi.org/10.1056/NEJMp13
11405)

Miscellaneous

Brain Health (https://www.alz.org/brain-health/brain_health_overview.asp)

Communication Skills (www.buzzle.com/articles/oral-communication-skills.html;
https://www.skillsyouneed.com/ips/communication-skills.html)

Differences Between Writing and Speech (http://www.omniglot.com/writing/writ
ingvspeech.htm)

Books and Short Stories

All the King's Men by Robert Penn Warren
The Call of the Wild by Jack London
The Canterbury Tales by Geoffrey Chaucer
The Cask of Amontillado by Edgar Allan Poe
The Catcher in the Rye by J. D. Salinger
Charlotte's Web by E. B. White
The Complete Works of William Shakespeare (Knickerbocker Classics) by William
Shakespeare

The Death of the Heart by Elizabeth Bowen

The Giving Tree by Shel Silverstein

Go Set a Watchman: A Novel by Harper Lee

Gone with the Wind by Margaret Mitchell

The Grapes of Wrath by John Steinbeck

Great Expectations by Charles Dickens

The Great Gatsby by F. Scott Fitzgerald

Huckleberry Finn by Mark Twain

If You Are Riding a Horse and It Dies, Get Off by Jim Grant and Char Forsten

The Iliad by Homer

The Indian in the Cupboard by Lynne Reid Banks

Jane Eyre by Charlotte Brontë

Leaves of Grass by Walt Whitman

The Legend of Sleepy Hollow by Washington Irving

Little Women by Louisa May Alcott

Lord of the Flies by William Golding

The Lord of the Rings by J. R. R. Tolkien

The Masque of the Red Death by Edgar Allan Poe

Moby-Dick by Herman Melville

My Favorite Time of Year by Susan Pearson

The Odyssey by Homer

Of Mice and Men by John Steinbeck

The Old Man and the Sea by Ernest Hemingway

Oliver Twist by Charles Dickens

Pride and Prejudice by Jane Austen

The Scarlet Letter by Nathaniel Hawthorne

The Scarlet Pimpernel by Baroness Emmuska Orczy

Seriously, Cinderella Is So Annoying!: The Story of Cinderella as Told by the Wicked Stepmother (The Other Side of the Story) by Trisha Speed Shaskan and Gerald Claude Guerlais

The Silly Story of Goldie Locks and the Three Squares (Hello Math Reader; Level 2) by Grace MacCarone and Anne Kennedy

Shakespeare's Sonnets by William Shakespeare

A Tale of Two Cities by Charles Dickens

The Tell-Tale Heart by Edgar Allan Poe
Ten Black Dots by Donald Crews
Terrifying Tales by Edgar Allan Poe
The Three Little Wolves and the Big Bad Pig by Eugene Trivizas and Helen Oxenbury
Three Men in a Boat by Jerome K. Jerome
Twelve Plays by Shakespeare (Dover Thrift Edition) by William Shakespeare
To Kill a Mockingbird by Harper Lee
The True Story of the Three Little Pigs by Jon Scieszka and Lane Smith
The Velveteen Rabbit by Margery Williams and William Nicholson
Wuthering Heights by Emily Brontë

Poetry

"Ages and Ages Returning at Intervals" by Walt Whitman
"Alone" by Edgar Allan Poe
"Beaches" by Kaitlyn Guenther
"A Dream Within a Dream" by Edgar Allan Poe
Haiku: This Other World by Richard Wright
"Gerontion" by T. S. Elliot
"The Happiest Day" by Edgar Allan Poe
"The Haunted Palace" by Edgar Allan Poe
"I Sing the Body Electric" by Walt Whitman
"Morning at the Window" by T. S. Elliot
"Nothing Gold Can Stay" by Robert Frost
"October" by Robert Frost
"Ode to Beauty" by Ralph Waldo Emerson
The Poetry of Robert Frost: The Collected Poems, Complete and Unabridged (Owl Book) by Robert Frost and Edward Cannery Lathem
"Preludes" by T. S. Elliot
"The Raven" by Edgar Allan Poe
"Rhapsody on a Windy Night" by T. S. Elliot
Robert Frost: Collection of 90 Poems with Analysis of Works and Historical Background (Annotated and Illustrated) by Robert Frost

"The Snow Storm" by Ralph Waldo Emerson
"Song of Myself" by Walt Whitman
"Spring Is in the Air" by Kaitlyn Guenther
"Winter" by Jim Milks

Paintings

Autumn in New England by Maurice Prendergast
A Carnival Evening by Henri Rousseau
The Dream by Henri Rousseau
Flowers in a Vase by Pierre-Auguste Renoir
I and the Village by Marc Chagall
Les Parapluies (The Umbrellas) by Pierre-Auguste Renoir
A Rain Shower by Ellen Trotzig
Starry Night by Vincent van Gogh
Spring by Joaquin Mir
Water Lilies (Nymphéas) series by Claude Monet

About the Author

An educator for more than 30 years, Denise L. Calhoun is National Board certified as a distinguished teacher in language arts. She holds a master's degree in educational psychology from California State University, Northridge; a teaching credential from the Graduate Department of Education at the University of California, Los Angeles; and a bachelor's degree in history from the University of California, Los Angeles. Calhoun mentors new teachers for the Los Angeles Unified School District and is a master teacher for California State University, Northridge, where she trains candidates in the credential program. Calhoun is currently pursuing her doctoral degree in organizational leadership from Pepperdine University's Graduate School of Education and Psychology. Her research explores the link between language and cognition and its implications for older adults.